WILLIAM E. ROGERS

Upon The Ways:
The Structure of
The Canterbury Tales

**ELS
EDITIONS**

© 1986 by William E. Rogers

ELS Editions
Department of English
University of Victoria
Victoria, BC
Canada V8W 3W1
www.elseditions.com

Founding Editor: Samuel L. Macey

General Editor: Luke Carson

Printed by CreateSpace

English literary studies monograph series
ISSN 0829-7681 ; 36
ISBN-10 0-920604-25-0
ISBN-13 978-0-920604-25-0

To Professor Norman E. Eliason

CONTENTS

PREFACE

Thanks are due Furman University for granting a sabbatical leave that made the writing of this monograph possible. I also thank the staff of the James B. Duke Library at Furman for their assistance with my research, and I am grateful to my colleagues for providing a congenial atmosphere to nourish scholarly inquiry. Especially, I am indebted to Dr. James T. Stewart of the English Department at Furman, who read and commented most helpfully on the manuscript.

Some of the theoretical concerns of this monograph are related to questions I took up in *The Three Genres and the Interpretation of Lyric* (Princeton, 1983). Specifically, the term *thematic* as I use it in this monograph corresponds with the term *epic* in the earlier study.

CHAPTER ONE

Manuscript Study of
The Canterbury Tales

In the last decades, most books about *The Canterbury Tales* have tried to see the work whole, to discover its coherence. Yet surely the task is hopeless, if seeing the work whole means knowing Chaucer's "final intention." Chaucer might not have arrived at anything we could reasonably call a "final intention." We grope in a cloud of manuscript variants and plausible assumptions, and we find out more about the structure of our own theories than we do about the structure of *The Canterbury Tales*. Nor does it help to resort to such concepts as "best evidence" and "most probable occurrence." These concepts merely imply that our conclusions always depend on conjectures. The crucial fact is always that we do not know what happened to Chaucer's manuscripts before or after his death. Nor, of course, will we ever know what Chaucer would have done had he lived to "finish" *The Canterbury Tales*.

Judged by its results for criticism, the inquiry into Chaucer's "final intention" has produced some interesting readings. It is historically important to know whatever we can about what Chaucer wrote and about transmission of medieval texts. But again and again the study of manuscripts as applied to the question of structure returns the same result—what we know is uninteresting or unhelpful, and what we want to know is precisely what we have to conjecture about. At last, critics close the circle by appealing to literary interpretations in arguing for some particular manuscript arrangement. Thus, manuscript study sometimes, almost as a side-effect, stimulates new readings. But if we want just new readings, we could order the fragments any way we please, and produce interpretations based on that order, without any reference to manuscript evidence.

I make these points not because manuscript study will be important in the sequel or because I think I can solve any of its problems. I want to make clear, instead, why I think manuscript study can be eliminated from the ground, pushed to the horizon of the critical exercise I plan to carry out.

Manly in 1931 concluded that manuscript evidence would not permit an argument for any "definite plan" on Chaucer's part;[1] over fifty years later, Charles A. Owen, Jr., writes that the fragments reflect "different stages" of Chaucer's plan.[2] And if there is emerging consensus about the ordering of *The Canterbury Tales*,[3] it is not based on manuscript evidence. Fifty years of study, in other words, have left us in much the same position, as regards the ordering of the tales. Why? Partly, I think, because of the nature of the beast; and partly because of our methods of pursuing it. The nature of the beast is to be reticent on certain essential points, about which we must then supply conjectures. All of the efforts to reconstruct the order of the tales from the geography of the pilgrimage,[4] for example, depend upon conjectures that Chaucer would or would not have revised or cancelled these geographical references if he had completed the work. But the work is unfinished. To say that a work is finished means, if it means anything, that the work corresponds as closely to the artist's conception of it as the artist himself judges that he can make it correspond. But the artist's own conception might evolve as he writes. Perhaps his final conception or "final intention" does not exist until the ultimate moment when by a lucky accidental stroke of execution he sees what he meant all along. And to say that a work is unfinished means precisely that it does not yet correspond to the artist's developing conception of it, and therefore that anything in it is subject to change. By the nature of the problem, not knowing what Chaucer would have done with the geographical references is the same thing as not knowing what tale-order he would have settled on. And we might as well conjecture about the latter as about the former.[5] The argument is not stronger for pretending that the airy interpretation is based on the "solider" manuscript evidence, when the manuscript evidence itself has been interpreted.

It is worth examining a bit more closely the structure of thought, or perhaps one should call it the methodology, that produces the kinds of arguments I am talking about. If one argues that fragment VII (B²) can be positioned by taking into account its relations with the Marriage Group;[6] or that the Ellesmere order can be supported by demonstrating how the Wife's performance is an answer to the Man of Law's tale;[7] or that the "floating fragment" (VI) can be fixed by noting thematic similarities between the Franklin's tale and the Physician's tale,[8] one inevitably draws the manuscript evidence itself into the hermeneutic circle. Instead of having unambiguous manuscript evidence upon which to base interpretive decisions, we find interpretive decisions used as evidence to accept or reject the ordering of "good" manuscripts. That there is a Marriage Group as traditionally conceived is a debatable interpretive decision.[9] That the Wife answers the Man of Law, or that the Physician alludes to the Franklin, is an interpretive decision. The methodology assumes that what we want is to recover the "Chaucerian" ordering, to know, if not Chaucer's "final intention," at least his intention at the last moment he was working on *The Canterbury Tales*. The interpretive process is complete, in this structure of thought, when we reach a definite decision about what was most probably in Chaucer's mind.

This kind of argument is more subtle than the argument that supplies leaves, fascicles, bound manuscripts, Chaucer's chest, editors and scribes as needed to account for the manuscript variants. One appears to treat the text (and manuscripts) as data and the interpretation as hypothesis. That is, one accounts for the genesis of the text, and ultimately for all the manuscript variants, by hypothesizing some particular intention in Chaucer's mind. One supports the hypothesis by showing how it might account for the data. One "explains" why Chaucer wrote what he wrote, how the physical text got produced. And one alters the hypothesis whenever it is inconsistent with the data. Then, once the hypothesis has been confirmed by more or less "clear" data—e.g., the clear text of the individual tales—one can use the hypothesis to bring into focus data that are not so clear—e.g., the ordering of the fragments. When one has the confirmed hypothesis, one has an interpretation of *The Canterbury Tales*, which is just a statement of "how it must have been" in Chaucer's mind when he stopped work.

Why does the quasi-scientific rigor of this methodology not produce agreement? It is precisely because the supposedly "clear" data are not really "clear." Hypotheses, as statements of cause, have to be correlated with objects—objects which are, in this case, the surviving manuscripts of *The Canterbury Tales*. To make this correlation, we work from interpretations of individual tales, as if those interpretations were "clear." But, especially if one favors the "dramatic" readings prevalent since Kittredge, the interpretation of any particular tale in *The Canterbury Tales* depends crucially on its relation to other tales. For example, if the Wife of Bath's performance comes after the Man of Law's (Ellesmere order), we can read the theme of feminine *maistrie* as the Wife's argument against Constance's feminine passivity. But if the Wife's performance comes before the Man of Law's (Hengwrt order), this particular interpretive possibility vanishes. Thus, the interpretation can be "clear" only after one has already made a decision about tale-order. If we insist that we are producing knowledge about the objects in the manner of the natural sciences, we make the hermeneutic circle vicious. We can have many different hypotheses accounting for the observed motions of the stars and planets; and we can *decide* among the hypotheses—but only if

11

we agree about what motions we actually observe. Our hypotheses accounting for the ordering of Chaucer's tales in the manuscripts are undecidable, because, not knowing how the tales are supposed to be ordered, we cannot agree about how any one of them is to be read.

I do not intend to reject the hypothetical method entirely as a means of inquiry in the human studies. It seems a legitimate method precisely to the extent that the concept of causation is legitimately applied to the solution of historical questions. But this method of pursuing "Chaucer's intention" through the manuscripts is bound to produce a series of undecidable hypotheses—precisely because we begin by admitting that the work is unfinished. I hope I have shown why it is legitimate to clear the ground of manuscript study when one is discussing the ordering of the fragments of *The Canterbury Tales*. Certainly the manuscripts tell us *something* about ordering. No one disputes that the tales of certain fragments belong together. Ultimately, whatever we do know about the text of *The Canterbury Tales* depends, in a more or less complex way, upon the manuscripts. But I am arguing that in an attempt to see *The Canterbury Tales* whole, it makes sense to push manuscript study to the horizon, where it remains as a limit but does not intrude upon the ground of interpretation.

Now that the ground is cleared, what sort of interpretation is appropriate? There seems to be little hope now of determining a "correct" ordering of the fragments, if "correct" means "Chaucerian." We would have to despair if we think of interpretation as the name of a process or program by means of which we arrive at some result that is the sole justification of the process. But there is another view of literary interpretation. We can think of interpretation as an on-going activity in which we continue to articulate our developing understanding of literary works. "We" means first of all each of us as individuals, and then all of us as a group, a school, an age, and finally a civilization. The fruit of the activity would not be definite knowledge of what went on in some author's mind six hundred years ago, but instead increased explicitness of our understanding of the literary works that the author left behind.

The history of Chaucer criticism bears out the view of interpretation as on-going activity. Every age and every decade seem to want to re-interpret Chaucer for themselves. As often in the study of medieval literature, we glimpse here a theoretical issue outlined in sharp clarity just because of the distance of the literature from our own time. The issue is that of the difference between the historical enterprise and the enterprise of literary interpretation. The two enterprises, though we might willfully mingle them or accidentally confuse them, are not necessarily the same. The difference is fortunate for my inquiry. We must choose first whether to interpret or to remain silent. If we insist that history and interpretation are the same, that the goal of interpretation is a statement about the intention of a certain historical figure, then I think we must remain silent on the question of the ordering of *The Canterbury Tales*. Even if we speculate, and admit we are doing it, we have already passed from a discussion of Chaucer to a discussion of ourselves and our own prejudices and rules of evidence—that is, of our interpretive systems.

But if, on the other hand, we think of interpretation as precisely an unfolding of our own interpretive systems, with the literary work as necessary correlate, the "matter" upon which our systems impose "form," then we are freed to interpret *The Canterbury Tales* whole. It would be something like looking through a kaleidoscope. The fragments of *The Canterbury Tales* are the richly colored bits and pieces of glass that, reflected in the system of mirrors that is our interpretive system, produce the design we see. And we are always aware that if we turn the kaleidoscope or shake our hand, we shall see a different design; and such knowledge is an inseparable part of our experience. And what is the value of approaching *The Canterbury Tales* this way? It is to reveal clearly and explicitly what those who continue to squabble about the "correct" manuscript order have already glimpsed confusedly. Part of what is to be understood about the bits and pieces, in fact the most interesting thing to be understood about them, is precisely their potential for entering into particular relations with other bits and with the reflecting structures. We might gain a sort of "scientific" knowledge of the bits of glass in a kaleidoscope by breaking into the cylinder and pouring out the chips, grown ugly and dull. But that is not the kind of knowledge we want. Placing the fragments of *The Canterbury Tales* into relation with each other, even though we cannot meaningfully speak of any *single* one of those relations as historically "correct," is a way of understanding each fragment more fully by understanding its possibilities. That is the kind of understanding we get in the human studies, and that is the justification, if any is possible, for attempting to see *The Canterbury Tales* whole.

CHAPTER TWO

Dramatic and Thematic Readings of *The Canterbury Tales*

As I suggested, critics today are making a conscious attempt to see *The Canterbury Tales* as a coherent whole. But of course, there have been gestures in that direction since Kittredge. I shall oversimplify, and say that there are two major ways of seeing *The Canterbury Tales* whole. One way is to read the work as drama, controlled by dramatic interactions among the pilgrims. This way regards the tales as dramatic speeches by the pilgrims. Another way is to read the work thematically, as controlled by Chaucer's own concern for certain recurring themes. This way regards the tales as varying sorts of statements about those themes. Either approach may be made to serve the other—critics might discuss themes in order to make points about the character of one of the pilgrims, and critics might discuss dramatic interactions in order to determine what statement Chaucer might be making about a particular theme. But there has been a noticeable shift in the direction of Chaucer criticism in about the last three decades, from a preoccupation with dramatic readings to a preoccupation with thematic readings. At one end of this period we find criticism that proceeds from Kittredge's assumptions—as, for example, the work of R. M. Lumiansky;[1] at the other end we find books such as Helen Cooper's *The Structure of the Canterbury Tales*, which suggests that the various stories are linked by Chaucer's "concern to bring out a number of interrelated themes in them, to set up a pattern of multiple perspectives," so that there is a "kind of cobweb effect, of lines of contact going off in a number of directions from any given point."[2] All of these critics are looking through their respective kaleidoscopes, but some of those in the last decade have seemed more aware that they are doing so.

Modern criticism concerning the structure of *The Canterbury Tales* begins with G. L. Kittredge's enormously influential remarks on the Marriage Group.[3] Critics today still accept the unity of fragments III-IV-V as a Marriage Group, with "interludes," and some of the best modern criticism of Chaucer has resulted from this assumption.[4] A great deal of criticism since Kittredge has either discussed the implications of Kittredge's Marriage Group, or attempted to extend the Group to include other tales.[5] To suppose that there is a Marriage Group is, as Kittredge himself very clearly points out, to regard the work as a drama and the pilgrims as *dramatis personae*.[6] Few books have gone further than Lumiansky's *Of Sondry Folk* (1955) in applying a thoroughgoing dramatic reading, however.

Perhaps we can call Ralph Baldwin's important monograph[7] a kind of turning point in Chaucer criticism. Published in the same year as Lumiansky's book, Baldwin's monograph seemed to open new possibilities for interpretation of *The Canterbury Tales* seen whole. Baldwin's purpose is to argue that a *thematic* concern—the theme of pilgrimage—holds the work together. From here it is not exactly a short step, but at least a more or less straight and continuous path, to the works of D. W. Robertson, Jr.,[8] and Bernard F. Huppé.[9] Much has been written both for and against "historical criticism," or "Patristic exegesis," or "Robertsonianism."[10] I shall merely observe two things: first, that historical criticism finds the unity of *The Canterbury Tales* in the moral lesson of *caritas*, a thematic reading; second, that the method of historical criticism is to read *The Canterbury Tales* by placing the work in the context of something else—in this case, loosely speaking, the works of the Church Fathers. The attempt to understand *The Canterbury Tales* by comparing them to something else, by "placing them in context," has become a major theme of Chaucer criticism.

This attempt tends to be opposed to dramatic readings of the tales. When we read the tales dramatically, we tend to assume that the pilgrims are people much like ourselves, interacting much as we should interact in their places, and that we have a natural or at least deeply ingrained cultural understanding of human interactions that is enough to enable us to understand the work. That is, if the work is "about" the interactions of people, we think we should be able to understand it fundamentally, if not in all its details, without resorting to a study of the "medieval mind." But if we resort to such a study, we seem to be assuming that the work is not "about" the interactions of people. Instead, it may be "about" structures of thought that are more or less alien to us, and that we must recover laboriously. Perhaps it has not been fully understood how deeply Kittredge's critical impulse differs from Robertson's. The difference is important. It might be defensible to combine dramatic and thematic readings in various ways, but when we fail to see how fundamentally the dramatic orientation toward the work differs from the thematic orientation, we generate confusion, and undecidable controversies proliferate in which each side thinks the other is being merely perverse.

Critics such as Robert Jordan[11] and Trevor Whittock[12] who consciously adopt a thematic orientation to *The Canterbury Tales* are especially concerned with the interaction between reader and text. Jordan, for example, specifically condemns approaching the work as drama, because to do so misses "the subtle play of human relationships between ourselves and the lively-minded poet" (p. 123) in which Chaucer "continually, and in varying ways, calls attention to the boundaries of the fiction" (p. 125). Implicit in such statements is a strong sense of generic difference. To read a work thematically is to regard it as a different kind of thing from the work that one reads dramatically. In thematic reading, the interaction between the reader and the "author" postulated in the interpretation and implied by the text moves forward to occupy the center of interest. That is not so when one reads a work dramatically. The dramatist is not found "in" his work, except perhaps as a fictional *persona* like Chaucer-pilgrim. The dramatist's mind underlies, underwrites the world he creates, but he does not become available as a commentator on that world. His mind is its reticent horizon, only that which we infer from the world he presents to us. But when a critic reads *The Canterbury Tales* thematically, he finds "Chaucer's mind" in every line, commenting, teasing, instructing, interacting with the reader.

In fact, the interaction between text and reader has become a major theme in the most recent criticism of *The Canterbury Tales*. That is not surprising, considering the popularity of "reader-oriented" or "reader-response" criticism. What is perhaps not so obvious is the intimate connection between the new concern for interaction between text and reader and the new concern for genre in Chaucer criticism.[13] The best book of recent years on *The Canterbury Tales* joins these two concerns. The book is Donald R. Howard's *The Idea of the Canterbury Tales* (1976), a definitive argument that it is possible to read *The Canterbury Tales* thematically, and a brilliantly worked out, though not definitive, statement of what it means to read the work that way. Howard's supposition that the work is *"unfinished but complete"*[14] frees him from the inherent disadvantage of all dramatic readings. The "drama" theory must suppose that the work is very far from complete, because there are just too many things that do not link up clearly in a dramatic way.

We find in Howard's book the explicitly articulated assumption that *The Canterbury Tales* is to be approached as a structure of thought, through the interplay between narrator and reader. Chaucer's mind moves from the horizon to the center of the stage. "At base," Howard says, the form of the work is that of "a memory," first "presented as the narrator's own, and the narrator is identified with the author...." But finally "We experience a memory of others' memories and thus lapse into a mentalistic realm" (pp. 188-89). Howard's discussion of the

16

"bookness" of *The Canterbury Tales*, similarly, makes the point that the work exemplifies a "new attitude toward reading" which is "the real heart of humanism": reading becomes a "voyage of exploration, writing a creation of worlds . . . in which the reader travels," an "interior world, a world drawn from other books, memory, and imagination, which can only exist as it takes shape in memory" (pp. 66-67). This "reading" is of course quite different from regarding *The Canterbury Tales* as a drama performed before our eyes on the road to Canterbury.

Howard's deep concern for genre proceeds from his perception that if the reader is to interact properly with the text, if he is to go on those voyages of interior exploration, he must have some notion of *what* he is confronted with. Howard spends a good deal of time discussing *The Canterbury Tales* as a *comedy*, and attempting to determine what Chaucer might have meant by the term. Howard concludes that Chaucer thought of a comedy as "a satiric and ironical work without the character of 'complaint' literature . . ." (p. 67). Thus *comedy* for Chaucer (and for Howard) does not have the dramatic connotation usual now. Howard makes the point more fully and more clearly than most other critics that if we mean to approach *The Canterbury Tales* as a work "about" a structure of thought, instead of familiar human interactions, we shall have to make some decision about what sort of structure of thought we have before us. We can make this decision consciously or unconsciously, but the decision gets made whenever an interpretation of *The Canterbury Tales* is written.

Howard's avowedly historical approach and his claims of historical correctness (" 'Then you are making the outrageous claim that you have seen into the mind of Geoffrey Chaucer?' Well, I am. But I say it isn't so outrageous"—p. 17) have perhaps obscured the fact that he actually has more in common with reader-oriented critics than with historical critics. Thematic readings of *The Canterbury Tales* often proceed by placing the work in the context of something else—the Church Fathers (Robertson and Huppé); or the Gothic cathedral (Jordan); or ancient and medieval story-collections (Cooper); or even the medieval commentaries on the poetry of Ovid (Judson Boyce Allen and Theresa Anne Moritz[15]). We find a similar impulse in Howard when he compares the form of *The Canterbury Tales* to the form of the initial capital in a medieval Psalter, or to a flower or rose window or *rota* (wheel) design, or to the form of "pilgrimage in retrospect" (p. 196). Admittedly, Howard does not mean flowers or pilgrimages as we might understand them now, but as they were understood in the Middle Ages—he spends many pages explaining just how these forms were understood. And he suggests that Chaucer got the idea for his "interlaced thematic structure" from the romances and dream-visions of his time (p. 225). But these images or models selected from the store of Howard's vast knowledge of the Middle Ages become simply ways of articulating the (informed) reader's interaction with the text. It is more significant that Howard's "trump card" in his book, the ultimate model in terms of which he wishes us to understand the structure of *The Canterbury Tales*, is precisely the model that allows the most room for the reader to enter into the construction of the meaning of the text. It is the model of the "medieval visual design called a labyrinth or maze" (p. 327). Howard's model is not a placeless labyrinth with no reference points, but a maze with a beginning and an end. Still, though, the maze must *be made sense of*, and it must be made sense of by the one who walks it—in this model, the reader. In her review of Howard's book, Florence Ridley seems to agree with me that Howard's approach, however much it claims to be historical, is at base reader-oriented. She says, "we may accept this book as a brilliant construct upon the *Canterbury Tales*, a result of collaboration between a fluent, highly informed, imaginative critic of the twentieth century and a literary genius of the fourteenth. . . ."[16]

None of this is said to diminish Howard's accomplishment. No critic completely escapes the currents of his time, and we are in a time when historical understanding itself seems to us to be constituted as a sort of collaboration or dialogue between the object of understanding and the one who understands. The stance of critics in Kittredge's day was perhaps different—literature, imitating objects in the world, itself became an object to be known as objects are known, "objectively." The dramatic readings of *The Canterbury Tales* fit this presupposition well. The work could be known as mimesis of something (human interactions), already more or less well understood, and to know the work was to recover the "reality" it represented. For Howard, and for many others who read Chaucer today, the situation seems more complex. It is important to understand how the critical stance exemplified in Howard's work compels one to consider as essential certain issues that are subordinate in a dramatic reading of the work. If we want to be clear-headed about what we are doing, we have to articulate clearly the differences between reading the work dramatically and reading it thematically. Failure to articulate those differences leads to confusion and pseudo-controversies.

One such pseudo-controversy, and the only one I shall consider here, is the on-going debate about the Chaucerian narrator. E. T. Donaldson began it in his essay "Chaucer the Pilgrim,"[17] by distinguishing between Chaucer-pilgrim and Chaucer-poet. John Major questioned the distinction, presenting "the Narrator as a kind of *alter ego* of the poet himself,

18

with just so many shades of difference as allow for ironic play...."[18] How many narrators are there, "really"? I think we can answer this question only by considering what Donaldson wanted to do with his distinction. He wanted to allow for both dramatic and thematic readings of *The Canterbury Tales*. We have a narrator who is a character, a *dramatis persona*, part of the world represented on the stage of the pilgrimage, and so we can have dramatic readings like Kittredge's. But we also have a narrator who is an author, the judge of the world he creates, and so we can have thematic readings in which the source of our interest is not so much the interactions among the pilgrims as it is the play of Chaucer-poet's mind upon his microcosm. As Donaldson says, the most obvious function of the Chaucer-pilgrim *persona* is "to present a vision of the social world imposed on one of the moral world" (p. 9). The vision of the social world is dramatic, that of the moral world necessarily thematic. Major, on the other hand, sees Chaucer-pilgrim as a "*persona* whose outlook is almost indistinguishable from Chaucer's own," a "marvelously alert, ironic, facetious master of every situation" (p. 162). That is, the source of interest in the passages where the narrator is prominent is precisely the play of the narrator's (Chaucer's) mind—a thematic reading.

The answer to whether the narrator is singular or plural is that both critics are right in terms of the readings they wish to adopt. If we are interested primarily in the play of Chaucer's mind, as Major is, then we need only one narrator—and we are reading the work thematically, as a structure of thought in some mind. If, on the other hand, we want to read the work as a presentation of a self-subsistent world—to apprehend it, in short, as drama—then we need a character, "Chaucer-pilgrim," to be a part of that world in a way its creator, "Chaucer-author," cannot be. Our understanding of the work, as always in a dramatic reading, somehow goes beyond anything we can attribute to any *persona*, and so we postulate an author at the horizon of the dramatic world. Entities multiply because of a decision about how to read the work—perhaps even an unconscious decision, in some cases—and not because there is any empirical way of "counting" the narrators.

A more recent version of the same debate arises from Howard's concept of "unimpersonated artistry." Howard refers to those places where "Chaucer's" voice apparently intrudes to drown out the pilgrim who is speaking, as for example in several places in the Knight's tale (p. 232). Howard's distinction is closely related to Donaldson's, though Howard is concerned to extend the application of the distinction beyond the frame-story and into the individual tales. H. Marshall Leicester, Jr., quarrels with the concept of "unimpersonated artistry," because the notion "puts us in the difficult position of trying to decide which parts of a single narrative are to be assigned to the pilgrim teller and which to the 'author.'"[19] Leicester explicitly recognizes that the debate is, at least in part, about whether *The Canterbury Tales* should be read dramatically. He argues that the work is not *just* dramatic, as Lumiansky and others have implied, but has instead an "insistent, though perhaps intermittent, *textuality*... the work repeatedly breaks the fiction of spoken discourse and the illusion of the frame to call attention to itself as a written thing" (p. 216). The speaker is not so much the creator of the text; instead, "The speaker is created by the text itself as a structure of linguistic relationships" (p. 217). Howard's notion of "unimpersonated artistry" seems to have a purpose similar to that of Donaldson's distinction between Chaucer-pilgrim and Chaucer-author, though the emphasis is different in the two cases. Donaldson seems to want to explain how a moral vision, or our apparently clear sense of Chaucer's mind, is consistent with a dramatic reading of *The Canterbury Tales*. Howard seems to want to explain how the drama we find in the *The Canterbury Tales* is consistent with a thematic reading. The difference in emphasis is symptomatic of the progress of Chaucer criticism since Donaldson's essay.

But again, the question of how many narrators there "really" are is moot. The question is, rather, how we are going to articulate our understanding of *The Canterbury Tales*. Are we going to allow room for the vocabulary we use to talk about drama, about speeches made by self-subsistent characters on a stage from which the creator absents himself? If so, we need to allow for a doubleness of voice, for two (or more) narrators. But if we see the poem as Leicester does, we are not looking at the self-subsistent world on the stage. Instead, we are examining a structure of thought embodied in a text: we attempt "to see from another's point of view, to stretch and extend the self by learning to speak in the voices of others" (p. 221). Then, we need only the one speaker, who is "as fictional as the pilgrims, in the sense that like them he is a self-constructing voice. He practices... the art of impersonation, finally, to impersonate himself, to create himself as fully as he can in his work" (p. 222). To attempt to understand that self thus created is precisely what it means to read *The Canterbury Tales* thematically.

Part of such a "modern" reading of Chaucer involves the willingness to approach *The Canterbury Tales* as a kind of meta-poetry, a writing about writing.[20] If we are interested in the mind embodied in the text, we are also interested in that mind's awareness of its own activity in producing the text. This preoccupation in Chaucer criticism suits the modern conviction that all poetry is on some level about poetry, and that all texts ultimately reveal their own inadequacy as representations of anything outside themselves. In the last decade a spate of studies has appeared attempting to define Chaucer's attitude toward poetry, and toward the possibilities of language.[21] It is possible to attribute this recent interest in the meta-poetry of *The Canterbury Tales* to the currents now fashionable in literary theory. But one might also regard it as a kind of flowering of the attempt to read *The Canterbury Tales* thematically, to see the work whole by attempting to define the quality of the narrating mind. Only in a thematic reading of *The Canterbury Tales* could the concern for meta-linguistic statement become part of the foreground in interpretation.

I mean to argue, then, that the concern for the interaction between the reader's mind and the poet's mind as embodied in the text, and the concern for *The Canterbury Tales* as meta-poetry, arise at least partly as the result of a decision about genre. We read *The Canterbury Tales* as drama, or we read it as something else. So far, I have lumped all the possibilities for "something else" under the heading of "thematic readings," but of course there are many different kinds of thematic readings, which regard the work as many different things. For that very reason, I am not especially fond of the term *thematic*. But that is the term currently immanent in Chaucer criticism that stands in opposition to *dramatic*, and so I use that term here in that way. I hope that as a result of my discussion the term *thematic* itself might emerge into greater clarity and explicitness. The opposition between "dramatic" and "thematic" is a crucial one for interpretation, and all the more so because the decision about how to read often seems to be made only implicitly. I have argued already that controversy about the plurality of narrators arises because of different generic emphases. I shall soon suggest that controversy about individual tales arises often because some critics want to read the tales dramatically, and some thematically. There is no settling such controversies, because both answers are "right." The tales can be read either way. All we can do is to make our assumptions explicit and thus dissolve the pseudo-controversy. The very activity of pursuing an interpretation makes us regard *The Canterbury Tales* as an object existing just as it is, apart from anyone's knowledge of it. But that assumption does not mean that *The Canterbury Tales* is an object like the "object" of the natural sciences. The objects of the human studies are not objects in this sense, at all. An essential aspect of the objects of the human studies is *meaning*. We "have" these objects, if at all, through our interpretations of them. The elementary error in the human studies is to confuse the interpretation with the "thing itself." When that confusion is cleared up, many pseudo-controversies dissolve.

To know what something *means*, we must already have some general idea of "what sort of thing it is." Otherwise, it remains unintelligible. Because we must enter the hermeneutic circle in all cases whatsoever of understanding of cultural objects, our generic sense of cultural objects often remains transparent to us. That generic sense involves a presupposition, a decision as it were, that lies below the level of explicit interpretation. We locate that decision only in retrospect, by analysis of our interpretation to disclose the tacit rules that govern it. The decision about whether to read *The Canterbury Tales* dramatically or thematically has often been just such a decision. After an interpretation is complete, we can reconstruct the decision that has determined it, articulate the decision, even produce arguments designed to show that *The Canterbury Tales* "really is" that sort of thing that we have taken it to be. But when we do produce such articulations or such arguments, we are merely reproducing the presuppositions that made us interpret *The Canterbury Tales* as we did in the first place. The value of articulating those presuppositions is precisely to dissolve controversies that are only apparent and to gain explicit understanding of our own interpretive systems.

Thus, it is important to deal explicitly with genre in any reading of *The Canterbury Tales* that sets out to be different from the traditional dramatic readings. And not *genre* just in the traditional sense of "literary type," but *genre* in a more fundamental sense, as that decision about what sort of thing a work is, that informs one's reading of the work at every stage of the interpretation. If *The Canterbury Tales* is not a drama, what is it? More specifically, since I am talking about structure, what sort of structure do we have?

For Howard, the structure is *retrospective*: "The work remembered makes us change our estimate of the work experienced" (p. 217); the work itself is a "labyrinth," an interlaced design associated with a "vicarious pilgrimage" (p. 332). By juxtaposition and concatenation the tales comment on each other, and the experience of the work is that of "obsolescence": "Ideals are in the past, actuality in the narrative 'now.' . . . *The Canterbury Tales* gives us a picture of a disordered Christian society in a state of obsolescence, decline, and uncertainty: we do not know where it is headed" (p. 115). George R. Keiser suggests that the "particular brilliance" of Howard's idea for someone interested in reconciling his reading with manuscript evidence is that Howard's reading "makes serial order a minor issue."[22] Howard indicates certain preferences in ordering (p. 215), but he does seem to want to sidestep the vexed problem of the "correct" order of tales, by a generic presupposition that does not demand any *particular* structure.

But I think there is a theoretical confusion here. If we were dealing with a truly pathless, placeless labyrinth, then serial order would not be even a minor issue—it would be no issue at all. But in the kind of labyrinth Howard is talking about, the maze has a solution. It makes a very great difference what fork one takes; in fact, in the labyrinth on the floor of Chartres cathedral that Howard cites (his Figure 14, on page 328), there is only *one* path possible for one who stays in the maze. In such a labyrinth, serial order is the *crucial* issue. This point is not a quibble. In the sort of medieval design that Howard cites, the form of the design itself implies a unique serial ordering, or at least a definite set of correct orderings. In the genuinely placeless labyrinth, on the other hand, any order that existed would have to be imposed by the one wandering in it. This equivocation on the notion of "labyrinth" perhaps goes deep in Howard's thought, on the one hand returning the conclusion that there is a historically correct "idea" of *The Canterbury Tales*, and on the other hand returning the conclusion that the ordering of the tales is not a crucial issue.

Howard's answer to this objection, of course, would be his distinction between "form" and "structure" of a work: "'form' has always tended to suggest an image, pattern, or fixed idea, 'structure' to suggest a process by which parts have been put together" (p. 210). Form for Howard is that which makes structure possible, that in terms of which the assembling of parts (structuring) becomes intelligible. The "form" of the labyrinth, then, does not imply any *particular* "structure." But I am arguing that one of two things must be so: either (1) the labyrinth is one of the form of the pavement labyrinth at Chartres cathedral, in which case a particular—indeed, unique—structure is implied, and serial order of the tales is a crucial issue; or (2) the labyrinth is genuinely pathless, in which case the structure is the creation (in Howard's case, certainly, an ingenious and satisfying creation) of the critic.

I want to say, of course, that the second thing is the case—that we know form, if at all, through structure, and that with *The Canterbury Tales* we are not in a medieval labyrinth like the one in Chartres cathedral, but in a truly placeless labyrinth of modern critical theory. What value, in this modern labyrinth, do Howard's interesting discussions of medieval flowers, wheels, pilgrimages, romances, and mazes have? They have the value of showing, as Florence Ridley says in the review of Howard's book that I have already cited, that "these ideas *might* have been Chaucer's." They also have the value of serving as models that allow Howard to articulate his insights into the work, whether or not these ideas were Chaucer's. That is what any model might do, whether or not it is "medieval." That is what I hope my model does, and in fact I would argue that it is no less distinctively "medieval" and no more distinctively "modern" than Howard's.

I have been carrying on, then, a submerged argument for critical pluralism and for multiplicity of meaning, for the "God's plenty" that since Dryden has become a particularly annoying cliché among Chaucer critics. When I give a reading of *The Canterbury Tales*, I shall not argue that my reading "corrects" or "refines" Howard's. I shall instead be trying to demonstrate what I have been implying all along in discussing Howard's work—that his book is a milestone in Chaucer criticism because its explicitly articulated assumptions free us to produce a whole new family of readings, much as Kittredge's work did for an earlier generation. That Howard claims historical correctness is neither here nor there, in my view, because in my view the writing of literary interpretation is distinctively different from the writing of history. But whatever the merits or demerits of Howard's book, he gives us a new way of looking at *The Canterbury Tales*.

As I have said, one of the most important things we can observe in Howard's book is that the decision about genre, about "what sort of thing the work is," is crucial to any thematic reading. In articulating what sort of thing *The Canterbury Tales* is, I shall seek something a bit simpler and readier to hand than Howard's medieval flowers, romances, or mazes. The simplicity of my notion is not a decisive advantage in itself—the question is how well the notion permits one to articulate an understanding of *The Canterbury Tales* seen whole. My notion does have the advantage (again not decisive) of being specifically alluded to in the work itself, and of being immanent in a great deal of the criticism of *The Canterbury Tales* in this century. I find my principle in the first lines of the Parson's tale, whose "metaphorical drift" Paul Ruggiers,[23] along with the Parson himself, points out. Translating his text from Jeremiah, the Parson says, "Stondeth upon the weyes, and seeth and axeth of olde pathes (that is to seyn, of olde sentences) which is the goode wey, / and walketh in that wey, and ye shal fynde refresshynge for youre soules, etc." (X.76-77).[24] If these "olde sentences" refer also to the preceding tales, many of which are in fact full of "sentences" of various kinds that were "olde" for Chaucer in his translating or adapting of them, then the Parson is implying that each tale embodies a "way" of life, a distinctive stance toward the world—or, as I would prefer to say in that much-abused term cast up by the German idealist tradition, a "world-view." If we take the "metaphorical drift" of the Parson seriously here, we shall see *The Canterbury Tales* as a *collection of world-views*. And that is how I propose to see it. Each tale embodies a world-view which the speaker of

24

the poem (loosely, "Chaucer") inhabits for the duration of the tale; and then the speaker moves to a complementary or contrasting world-view.

This way of looking at *The Canterbury Tales* as a series of world-views is certainly implicit in Howard's notion of the work as a structure of juxtapositions and concatenations. It is certainly not far from the comment of H. Marshall Leicester, Jr., that I have already quoted, to the effect that the speaker of the work practices "the art of impersona-tion, finally, to impersonate himself, to create himself as fully as he can in his work." Or, as Alfred David says, "All of the Canterbury pilgrims are in some measure *personae* of Chaucer" (*The Strumpet Muse*, p. 158). The idea is not new, by any means. Paul Ruggiers reads *The Canterbury Tales* this way, anticipating Howard's work in several important respects. Ruggiers gives up the idea of finding a unified dramatic plot, and reads the tales as "a series of intellectual discoveries" presenting, when taken collectively, a "multifaceted view of experience" that is the meaning of the whole work (pp. xiv, 7).

In fact, the notion of the tales as somehow embodying world-views has been pervasive in Chaucer criticism of the last decade or so,[25] and the remarks of many critics are enough to suggest what the form of *The Canterbury Tales* must be, if the work is read as I intend to read it. That form is not a visual design or a literary genre, but instead a human response conceived as a cultural form, codified and sharable, as erotic experience is sharable in love-poetry or as religious experience is sharable in liturgy. That form is *dissatisfaction*. The motivation for the next tale or group of tales is always dissatisfaction with the world-view implicit in the last tale. Thus, this form implies a local structure. And I shall argue that the form is not transcended, that at the end of *The Canterbury Tales* we have not satisfaction, but a deeper dissatisfaction not only with the various ways of looking at the world, but with life itself as lived in a fallen world. And that dissatisfaction is at last salutary.

For those who are interested in bringing Chaucer's work into relation with other works of his age, I might mention that taking dissatisfaction as the form of *The Canterbury Tales* suggests deep similarities between Chaucer's work and the work of his two great contemporaries, the Gawain-poet and William Langland. *Sir Gawain and the Green Knight* has as main theme an attack on the self-satisfaction of Gawain and Arthur's court; the *Pearl* of course consists largely of the dreamer's reiterated expressions of dissatisfaction with his experience and with the arguments and injunctions of the Pearl-maiden. And perhaps the only entirely clear structuring principle of *Piers Plowman* is the repetition of the pattern in which the restless dreamer, receiving instruction of some sort, believes he understands the mysteries that goaded him, thus mounts into

25

pride, and then by experience or authority is rebuked for his presumption. But with such considerations aside, I pick dissatisfaction as the form of *The Canterbury Tales* because I think that notion, while simple and ready to hand, allows for adequate complexity in articulating the relations between the tales. Furthermore, the notion allows me to preserve what I find most valuable in contemporary Chaucer criticism, while also illuminating new possibilities in the relations between tales and highlighting themes previously underemphasized that I find to be crucial in the work.

To discuss structure, then, means to explain precisely how the succeeding tale or group of tales comments on the inadequacies in the world-view of the preceding tale or group of tales. The articulation of structure is the articulation of what the mind is dissatisfied with as it proceeds through the work. Is this dissatisfied mind Chaucer's? I do not know. My interpretive model does not require that it be Chaucer's mind. It might at worst be my own mind, or the mind of the Ellesmere editor, since I talk about the Ellesmere order. But that sort of knowledge is all one may expect in the human studies—increased understanding of one's own interpretive systems and, correlatively, more explicit understanding of the individual tales considered as sets of possibilities for entering into relations with other tales and with the interpretive system itself.

Looking at *The Canterbury Tales* as a series of world-views is not new. If I shall be able to make any claim for anything new in my approach, it will be that I hold more consciously and more rigorously than some others to an important distinction—the distinction between *saying* and *showing*. This distinction was made famous among philosophers by Ludwig Wittgenstein. But without attempting to plumb the distinction to the bottom of its philosophical profundity, I think it can be useful in talking about world-views embodied in stories. What a story *says* is not its world-view, even in cases such as Aesop's fables or a medieval allegory with a blatantly displayed *sentence*. Instead, what a story *shows* is its world-view. What is *shown* cannot be *said*, because all that a story says is predicated upon its world-view. The world-view of a story is transparent in the fictive world, transparent to its narrator. The Knight's tale says things about Theseus, Palamon, Arcite, Emelye, and the gods; it also says things about the theme of order. But it also *shows* things about order—largely through its own structuring—that add to, qualify, or even contradict what it says. This second level of meaning is what I am after when I talk about the world-view implicit in the tale. I ask, "What must be the nature of the world for this kind of story to exist? What world must the mind inhabit in order to dwell in this story, either as its creator

26

or as its reader?" And the structure of *The Canterbury Tales* is the movement of the mind as it proceeds, restless and dissatisfied, from one of its worlds to another.

In this study I shall abstract to a large extent from any consideration of the frame-story. My purpose is to talk about the ordering of the *tales*. But the frame-story itself of course embodies a world-view, one that opens the possibility of reading the whole work dramatically. So I shall, occasionally, talk about dramatic interactions, by way of showing how a thematic reading could incorporate the insights of dramatic readings and make those insights serve its own ends.

I have said that I shall talk about the Ellesmere order. I need not justify that choice, given my model of interpretation, but nevertheless I shall say a word about the choice. If one considers the boundary of my inquiry, the evidence of the manuscripts, it is still possible to argue that if the concept of "final intention" means anything, the Ellesmere order is the best representative of that final intention. (It is also possible to argue otherwise.) The decisive point, however, is that the Ellesmere order in my reading places the Pardoner's tale and the Nun's Priest's tale in positions suitably crucial for tales that have so often been called Chaucer's best, thus suggesting a new dimension in the complexity of these tales.

It remains, then, to read the tales.

CHAPTER THREE

Fragment I:
Social Order and Individual Freedom

The field of fragment I has been so thoroughly plowed, especially the plot of the Knight's tale, that many times a critic has only to locate himself in a particular spot within the range of critical opinion. It is a commonplace that the Miller parodies the Knight, and that the Reeve's performance is a less sporting rejoinder to the Miller.[1] Everybody finds a kind of "degenerative movement" (Howard's phrase) in the fragment. The successive narrators place less and less value on intellect,[2] vulgarity replaces refinement,[3] attitudes toward sex degenerate,[4] and the incomplete Cook's tale represents human life lived at the crudest and most meaningless level.[5]

Howard offers perhaps the best summary of the "degenerative movement" in fragment I: in the Knight's tale, "civil virtues give the characters and their actions dignity. But this civility is . . . an artifice. . . . To the Miller, civility is a mask for earthier, and to him healthier, motives; to the Reeve civility is a pure sham masking meanness and guile."[6] To find a degenerative movement in the fragment is of course to read the tales thematically, and the critics who find such a movement implicitly regard each of the tales as embodying a world-view that is more or less severely judged by the poet. Howard articulates the movement in the fragment in terms of a dialectic between "civility" on the one hand, and something else on the other—artifice in the Knight's tale, lust in the Miller's, and "meanness" in the Reeve's. I prefer to articulate the movement a little differently. What Howard calls "civility," I should call "social order"; and what he calls various names in the various tales, I should subsume under the heading of "individual freedom." Operating at this level of abstraction, one can see how essentially the same dialectic is working in all of the tales of the fragment. But more important for my purposes, one can see the precise sense in which the fragment represents a philosophical and linguistic failure. That is, the concept of "order," with its associated terms, and the concept of "freedom," with its associated terms, are erected in the fragment as an opposition whose purpose is to explain in a satisfying way the totality of human life. The

28

opposition proves inadequate, and that is precisely what the fragment *shows* without *saying*.

I want to maintain, then, that the general form of dissatisfaction is realized in fragment I in a structure generated out of the dialectic between order and freedom. Specifically, in the Knight's tale an attempt is made to construct a comprehensive social order that harmonizes with natural and divine orders, but the making of this attempt shows in sharp relief how human freedom is in this world-view too restricted for anyone to assent whole-heartedly to the world-view. In the Miller's tale, we see successful and unsuccessful attempts to manipulate social order to extend the range of individual freedom. The characters in the Reeve's tale try to restrict the range of others' freedom, and end up restricting their own, by the violent and perverse assertion of an invalid social order. And finally, in the little bit that we have of the Cook's tale, Chaucer already hints at the total breakdown of social order and the concomitant loss of meaning in the concept of individual freedom. Thus, in the Cook's tale we have an opposite to the Knight's tale. The Knight's tale is a finished, obviously patterned and highly wrought exposition of the idea of order and its implications for human freedom; the Cook's tale is an unfinished, colloquial ramble into a story that is apparently about a thoroughly disorderly situation where it does not make much sense to talk about human freedom. The successive dissatisfactions with the world-view of each tale culminate in a dissatisfaction with the whole fragment, and we are ready for a new beginning.

The Knight's Tale

No one doubts that the Knight's tale is about order—both social order and universal order. Critical controversy centers on how valid its vision of order is. That controversy, in turn, gravitates toward two related questions. First, to what extent does Chaucer (or, as some ask, the Knight himself) endorse the views and actions of Theseus, who seems to represent social order and who delivers the last word on universal order in the "First Mover" speech? Second, what is the place of Saturn in the poem? If Theseus' vision of the First Mover is valid, then Saturn must be just a subordinate part of the great chain of being, and his apparently disorderly effects on men must be the workings of a higher order. In this Boethian view, the relationship of Saturn to the First Mover would be something like the relation of Fortune, in a Christian theology, to God's Providence. If, on the other hand, Saturn is really the terrifying, disorderly force he sometimes seems to be, then his function in the poem is to qualify the validity of Theseus' vision.

29

These problems, I would like to suggest, are like the problem of how many "Chaucers" there are narrating *The Canterbury Tales*. They are pseudo-problems, arising because different decisions have been taken—often, it seems, unconsciously—about how to read the Knight's tale. Interpretations grounded in dramatic reading will produce different solutions than interpretations grounded in thematic reading. A dramatic reading asks the tale to tell us something about the mind of the Knight. Is the vision of order valid? Yes, it is valid, *if* we accept that vision as being grounded in the Knight's world-view *and* believe that Chaucer admires or endorses the Knight as ideal character in the drama. A thematic reading, on the other hand, questions the world-view of the tale itself. The tale itself becomes a structure of thought in some mind other than the Knight's (Chaucer's mind, the reader's mind). Is the vision of order valid? No, it is not, in the sense that it is grounded in only one of many possible world-views, each of which, because it is individual, is also limited. Controversies that arise because of our decisions to read the tale one way or the other are undecidable, because they are not controversies about "how things are." At bottom there is nothing to appeal to but a decision that the reader has made, often without being aware of it—there is nothing to appeal to but the structure of the interpretation itself.

Thus, we can explain why the critics who see the vision of order in the Knight's tale as valid and Theseus as the wise spokesman of that vision are also those who tend to read the tale dramatically. They are inquiring into the world-view of the tale as a world-view appropriate for the ideal Knight. Such critics might see the tale as a portrayal of the noble life;[7] or as the Boethian refutation of the errors that later surface in the philosophically inadequate Monk's tale, which the Knight stints;[8] or as the Knight's instruction of his son the Squire in the principles of Christian chivalry;[9] or a revelation of the Knight's own awareness, in his identification of himself with Theseus, that all attempts to impose order are doomed, but that the noble response is to continue to fight against disorder.[10] In all of these readings the tale either becomes a dramatic portrayal of the Knight's own character ("nobility"), or performs some dramatic function in the frame-story, or both. And in all of these readings, Theseus' vision is taken as corresponding to the Knight's vision, and as being valid and final in some sense. Saturn in dramatic readings becomes either a beneficent force misunderstood by limited human beings, a participant in a higher order;[11] or perhaps a representative of an old, strict, "inhuman" principle of ordering that has been supplanted by the reign of Jupiter and his representative Theseus.[12]

In thematic readings, on the other hand, critics might make Theseus himself aware of the inadequacies of his own vision;[13] or they might deny the validity of Theseus' vision while also denying Theseus' awareness of his own confusion;[14] or they might question in a more general way the "reality" of the world-view of the Knight's tale, pointing to lapses into low style or ironic or comic touches in the tale to prove that Chaucer does not fully endorse the vision embodied there.[15] Theseus, then, more or less deluded in his world-view, leaves Saturn out of account—Saturn, who represents arbitrary Fortune[16] or the stasis of death.[17] Rather than asking what the tale tells us about the Knight or what it contributes to the drama of the frame-story, these critics ask what we can learn from the tale about Chaucer's view of the world as distinct from the Knight's or Theseus'.

Joseph Westlund's reading of the Knight's tale, the reading closest to my own,[18] might almost serve as a paradigm of this sort of thematic reading. Westlund's essential point is that the world-view of the Knight's tale is *pagan*, with all that implies for its place in the Canterbury scheme and in Chaucer's own world-view. Westlund argues that Chaucer removes Christian overtones from his sources, and gives Theseus a *less* convincing argument for universal order than Boethius gives to Dame Philosophy (pp. 527, 533-36). Theseus' efforts to impose order are inadequate, and the gods themselves with their "partiality, willfulness, and strife" are "largely a reflection of the chaos inherent in life" (p. 532). Thus, the poem "raises problems which noble conduct cannot fully resolve, and it becomes increasingly difficult to assert a formal and judicious pattern of conduct" (p. 532). Westlund then sees the Knight's tale as an "impetus to pilgrimage."

There are, then, two distinct structures of interpretation of the Knight's tale, each coherent on its own assumptions. In one structure of interpretation, the tale seems to present a valid vision of universal order, subsuming the apparent disorder of society and of individual lives. In this view, human beings are free to choose the noble life, even in the face of acknowledged adversity, and to shape meaningful lives and orderly societies in the confidence that those lives and societies also have meaning in the inscrutable universal order. Saturn, in this view, represents not so much actual disorder as the limitation of human perception. The world of the tale is not explicitly Christian, but it is easily reconcilable with the Christian world-view. In another structure of interpretation, the tale seems to present a failed attempt to grapple with the problem of order, a deluded assertion of universal order in the face of the plain fact that social order and order in individual lives are impossible to maintain. In this second view, human freedom is problematic. Human beings are puppets of higher forces, and all humans ultimately die whether they want to or not. Saturn, in this second view, represents a terrible, even hostile principle of disorder before which human beings are both physically and intellectually helpless. The universe is ultimately unintelligible, and the world-view of the tale is irreducibly pagan.

I have associated the first structure of interpretation with dramatic readings of *The Canterbury Tales*. The implicit assumption is that because the Knight is an ideal character on the pilgrimage, Chaucer must to a large extent endorse his world-view. The tale is an expression of the character who utters it, and the primary control on the interpretation of the tale is the dramatic frame-story. The second structure of interpretation arises from an articulation of the tale as thematic. One entertains its world-view only as a system of thought in some mind—not necessarily one's own. The system of thought does reveal something about the Knight, but the Knight is not the center of interest. Instead, the center of interest is the relation of the world-view itself to some other system of thought. In some of the thematic readings, that other system of thought is the Parson's tale, or the "unromantic" later poetry of Chaucer, or medieval attitudes toward Fortune or toward the pagan world-view. In an interpretation of the structure of *The Canterbury Tales*, that different, inclusive system of thought is *The Canterbury Tales* itself seen whole. We must move outside the world-view of the tale, take it as an object in its own right and not as some sort of heuristic apparatus for understanding the Knight.

If I am right, the critical controversy implicit in the two structures of interpretation is a pseudo-controversy. It is undecidable because we have no way of knowing whether the Knight's tale "should" be read dramatically or thematically. Perhaps the situation would be different if the work were finished, but it is not finished. Perhaps even then, however, we could not decide. Part of the fundamental decision about "what sort of thing" *The Canterbury Tales* is is a decision about literary genre. And that decision grounds other interpretive decisions. What is crucial for individual interpretations and for the respectability of literary criticism as an intellectual discipline is that each critic should become aware of what his own interpretive decisions have been, and on what assumptions those interpretive decisions rest. We never "have" the work fully in any interpretive statement. The work is always just the "other pole" of the interpretive act.

To align myself with those who read the Knight's tale thematically, then, does not mean that I think the dramatic readings are "incorrect." I am saying only that *if* one reads *The Canterbury Tales* in a certain way—

the way that seems most promising, indeed, for seeing the work whole—
then one will have to see the Knight's tale, in general terms, as the
thematic readings see it. Furthermore, if the form of the whole work is
dissatisfaction, then we shall find something "in" the world-view of the
Knight's tale to prevent our resting in it, something dissatisfying about
it.

Having located myself on the critical spectrum, I should now like to
add a few remarks to the points that other thematic readings have
already made.

The world-view of the Knight's tale is what the tale shows about the
world. One of the most obvious things the tale exhibits is the general lack
of human freedom, and the inability of human beings to accomplish
what they intend. The characters in the tale also *say* something very
much like this in particular instances: "it may noon oother be. / Fortune
hath yeven us this adversitee" (1085-86).[19] But of course, what particular characters say is not decisive in determining what the tale shows,
because that saying itself must be judged in terms of the world-view of
the tale. Some of the thematic readings I have alluded to point out how
all of Theseus' attempts to impose order (except the last) result in more
disorder, and certainly Palamon and Arcite seldom seem in control of
their own destiny. Arcite is released from prison because "It happed on a
day" (1189) that Perotheus pleads for him, and he attributes the
situation to "aventure," Fortune (1235 ff.). Arcite returns to Athens
because Mercury urges him in a dream (1385 ff.)—he reminds one of
Troilus; one would have thought the idea might have occurred to him
on his own. Palamon escapes through "helpyng of a freend," but it is
"by aventure or destynee" (1465-68), and Arcite rides into the grove
where Palamon is hiding "By aventure" (1506). The great apostrophe to
"destinee, ministre general" has as its occasion Theseus' apparently
fortuitous decision to hunt in the same grove. Palamon is taken in the
tournament "By force" (2651), and Arcite's fall, caused by Saturn's
intervention, is attributed to bad luck: "For fallyng nys nat but an
aventure" (2722). Emelye's destiny is determined for her. And the
references throughout the tale to Fortune, destiny, "aventure," "cas" as
governors of human life are too numerous to list. In this light, Theseus'
advice "To maken vertu of necessitee" (3042) seems less exalted "wysdom" than a kind of bitter stoicism.

So the tale shows us a universe where human beings are free to have
intentions but not free to carry them out—even Theseus' best intention,
to make in the marriage "O parfit joye, lastynge everemo" (3072) is
obviously by his own admission doomed. The tale also shows us an
inherent contradiction in Theseus' own way of stating his vision of

33

universal order. As Theseus puts it, "The Firste Moevere" knew what he was doing: "For with that faire cheyne of love he bond / The fyr, the eyr, the water, and the lond / In certeyn boundes" (2991-93). Theseus' vision depends on two concepts: "love" and "degree." Love as a principle creates order by binding the elements into a structure according to their degree. The material order of the universe is closely associated in Theseus' mind with the social or cultural order. Not only does the wasting away of trees, stones, and rivers imply that limited duration of species is part of the overall order, but also "The grete tounes se we wane and wende. / Thanne may ye se that all this thyng hath ende" (3025-26).

But if we look elsewhere in the poem, we see a rather different statement about love and degree, this time the narrator's:

> O Cupide, out of alle charitee!
> O regne, that wolt no felawe have with thee!
> Ful sooth is seyd that love ne lordshipe
> Wol noght, his thankes, have no felaweship. (1623-26)

This proverbial wisdom is opposed to Theseus' neo-Platonic philosophical commonplace. And indeed, love in the Knight's tale is most often a disorderly force, on the level of human society. It causes the falling-out of Palamon and Arcite. Arcite defends himself against Palamon's charge of falseness by another proverb: "Wostow nat wel the olde clerkes sawe, / That 'who shal yeve a lovere any lawe?'" (1163-64) Theseus' love for Perotheus (1196-97) and Perotheus' love for Arcite (1202) bring about Arcite's release, thus destroying the neat balance between Arcite and Palamon achieved at line 1186, and triggering the gusty contesting laments about Fortune on the part of the young knights. Theseus, too, recognizes from experience the potential of love to become a disorderly force on the social level:

> And yet hath love, maugree hir eyen two,
> Broght hem hyder bothe for to dye.
> Now looketh, is nat that an heigh folye?
> Who may been a fool, but if he love? (1796-99)

The tale *says* both that love on one level is a force of order, and that love projected on the social level is often a force of disorder. But in *saying* that, the tale *shows* a paradox inherent in the world-view articulated there. The highest way of articulating a vision of order is by the use of the concept of love, and yet this very same concept is the highest way of articulating relationships between human beings that are ultimately disorderly. The tale shows us, in other words, a deficiency or inadequacy in this concept of love for the articulation of human experience. Love conceived as in the world-view of the tale is not a satisfactory universal principle. A higher principle, a different kind of love than mutual attraction of likes or repulsion of opposites, is needed.

There is a similar problem with the concept of sovereignty or degree. Theseus risks losing our sympathy at some points in the tale—once when he apparently casually and cruelly sends the young knights to prison, with no inquiry into their pasts or their personalities. The tale perhaps emphasizes his tyrannical behavior by the immediate reiteration of the crucial adjective *worthy*, here a touch ironical. Even the looters are kinder than Theseus:

> Out of the taas the pilours han hem torn,
> And han hem caried softe unto the tente
> Of Theseus; and he ful soone hem sente
> To Atthenes, to dwellen in prisoun
> Perpetuelly—he nolde no raunsoun.
> And whan this worthy duc hath thus ydon,
> He took his hoost, and hom he rit anon....   (1020-26)

We feel that Palamon's characterization of Theseus is not too strong, in his prayer to Venus (whom he imagines Emelye to be), when he speaks of the young knights' "lynage... / That is so lowe ybroght by tirannye" (1110-11). Again, and again with the reiterated "worthy," Theseus agrees all too readily with Palamon's suggestion that the young knights be executed. After Palamon's desperate speech, betraying himself and Arcite, one expects something better of Theseus' wisdom, but he again seems almost to play the tyrant:

> This worthy duc answerde anon agayn,
> And seyde, "This is a short conclusioun.
> Youre owene mouth, by youre confessioun,
> Hath dampned yow, and I wol it recorde;
> It nedeth noght to pyne yow with the corde.
> Ye shal be deed, by myghty Mars the rede!"   (1742-47)

The point is that Theseus in his "lordship" wants no "fellowship," any more than the lover wants fellowship in his love. Theseus' solution for the problem of the Theban women—to kill Creon and all of his followers in Thebes—is symptomatic. Degree is maintained by strenuous repression of those who challenge sovereignty. Thus, like love, degree is said to contribute to the universal order, but it becomes a force for disorder when projected on the social level. The tale shows us that the concept of degree, in its world-view, is insufficient to account for human experience. The chain of love is too much like the chains of the prison. The world-view that depends on Theseus' conception of the "faire cheyne of love" ultimately cannot grapple with all we know. We need a higher, better concept of sovereignty.

As I have suggested already, one could summarize by saying that the world-view of the Knight's tale is essentially *pagan*. The Knight's tale seems to me very like Dante's *Inferno* in its judging of the pagan world-view. Dante in the *Inferno* palpably judges the vision of Vergil's *Aeneid*. In the *Aeneid* evil appears as the enemy of order and civilization. Again and again, order is imposed by a terrible effort, a strenuous repressing of the forces of disorder—storms, giants, monsters, civil wars, individual passions. But those forces remain alive, thrashing and throbbing beneath the orderly surface, ready to erupt the moment the strenuous civilizing effort is relaxed. This is the world-view Dante judges when he refuses to allow his guide Vergil the beatific vision of perfect Love that transcends the mundane struggle between order and disorder, and when he portrays the manifestation of that Love in Hell as scornful *power*. I think the pagan world-view is similarly judged in the Knight's tale through Chaucer's use of the figure of Saturn. Saturn, by his positioning in this obviously structured artifice, represents on the divine level what Theseus represents on the human level. The major structural pattern of the poem is a simple one: there is a balanced presentation of competing forces, and then some other force steps in to restore order—ineffectively, for the pattern then repeats itself. The tale oscillates back and forth between Palamon and Arcite, with their symmetrical laments, their corresponding adventures, their followers at the tournament. Theseus normally steps in to end one conflict and inadvertently begin another: he ends the "Greet . . . strif" between the prisoners by releasing Arcite, but he begins another series of laments and puts in train the events leading to the tournament. Theseus stops the fight in the grove, but in fact only postpones the battle. Theseus even imposes order on the knights who follow Palamon and Arcite back to Athens: after the balanced descriptions of Lycurgus and Emetreus, we are told, Theseus "inned hem, everich at his degree" (2192).

But the structural pattern is elevated to the realm of the gods with the balanced descriptions of the three temples, the prayers, and the altercation between Mars and Venus. Here, though, Saturn steps in, first to postpone the resolution of the argument (2470 ff.) and finally to resolve the conflict by killing Arcite (2668 ff.). So the meticulous, "inorganic" patterning of the poem, to which the Knight and all critics constantly call attention, serves to focus sharply on Saturn as the representative of divine order. But what is Saturn? As everyone has pointed out, he is Fortune. His famous description of himself (2454 ff.) reminds almost irresistibly of some of the Old English "ubi sunt" passages where the scop laments the power of *wyrd* to destroy everything that is beautiful and meaningful in human life. All of the gods are hostile to men, as the decorations in their temples indicate. But Saturn, particularly, is hostile in a dark and secret way. No one knows why some are drowned and others spared, or why the walls fall on some and not others. Perhaps even the causes of "The murmure and the cherles rebellyng" seemed inscrutable in Chaucer's time, when, lacking a Marxist or even capitalist progressive view of history, educated men must have thought that the lot of the churls was much the same as it had always been. Certainly the causes of the pestilence were obscure, and thus appropriately attributed to a kind of Saturnian evil eye: "My lookyng is the fader of pestilence" (2469). Even the humanly attributable events that Saturn governs are touched with darkness and mystery: "the prison in the derke cote" (2457); "the pryvee empoysonyng" (2460); "The derke tresons, and the castes olde" (2468). The hostility of Fortune is ultimately inscrutable. That is the sum of pagan wisdom, and there pagan wisdom must rest. It can affirm faith in some higher order, but it can never hope to understand that order or to structure human life by intellect so as to participate in it. The universe is unintelligible, and ultimately, in the pagan world-view the universal order, if any, is hostile to men—for men die. Egeus tells Theseus as much with his examples of "Joye after wo, and wo after gladnesse" (2841)—the order here is significant. As Egeus says,

> This world nys but a thurghfare ful of wo,
> And we been pilgrymes, passynge to and fro.
> Deeth is an ende of every worldly soore.   (2847-49)

This observation might be a reason for "The peple that they sholde hem reconforte" (2852), but it is hard to see how it could be any comfort to Arcite. And so we must be left asking with him, "What is this world? what asketh men to have? / Now with his love, now in his colde grave" (2777-78).

The Knight's tale does not *say* these things about the pagan world-view. By its elaborate structuring it *shows* them. Thus, in the thematic structuring of *The Canterbury Tales* we have the first move in a dialectic between human freedom and social order. The Knight's tale shows us that the pagan world-view is not satisfying. We require a different idea of love, a different idea of sovereignty, and a different idea of order. The best that unaided human wisdom can do is attractive indeed, but it is not enough.

The Miller's tale is not a controversial tale. All the critics agree that it is in some sense a parody of the Knight's tale, as the Miller himself suggests when he says that he will "quite with the Knyghtes tale" (3119). Critics differ on what exactly is being parodied—courtly-love conventions,[20] chivalric ideals,[21] the elevated language of romance literature,[22] the passivity of the lovers in the Knight's tale,[23] civility,[24] learning[25]—and the answer is probably that the Miller's tale takes a swipe at all of these things. As we might expect, there is some question about how we are to judge the viewpoint embodied in the tale. After all, if the Miller's tale parodies the Knight's, and critics cannot agree about the validity of the viewpoint presented in the Knight's tale, it stands to reason that they should not be able to agree about the viewpoint that parodies that of the Knight's tale. But this question has not provoked nearly so much fruitful discussion as the corresponding question for the Knight's tale.[26]

The Miller does not attack the Knight's tale where it might seem most vulnerable—at the point where it fails to deal with the problem of evil. Instead, the Miller attacks at a point more dramatically appropriate to his character. What the tale shows is that the world is composed only of bodies, and that anyone who thinks otherwise is a fool. The Miller's tale engages a dialectic with the Knight in which the Miller takes the position that social order, such as it is, is just another manifestation of appetite.[27] The characters in the tale are free to create, subvert, or manipulate social order to satisfy their bodies, and that is what they all try to do, with more or less success. And they are right, in the world-view of the tale, for the tale "opposes itself to the tendency of the medieval mind to see physical objects and everyday events as outward signs of an invisible higher reality."[28]

All of the main characters in the tale illustrate the point, but none better than "hende Nicholas." His epithet, the subject of much commentary, suggests already in its punning that "graciousness" is nothing more nor less than being "handy" or "good with one's hands." Nicholas proves the principle in his wooing of Alisoun. Though he offers a vulgar parody of courtly-love language (3277-78), he is successful because of his hands: "he caughte hire by the queynte" (3276), "heeld hire harde by the haunchebones" (3279), "thakked hire aboute the lendes weel" (3304). Nicholas also uses various social institutions for his bodily pleasure. The institution of the university supports him in leisure: "this sweete clerk his tyme spente / After his freendes fyndyng and his rente" (3219-20). His pretended theological study allows him to fool John and Alisoun; he invokes John's superstitious fear of his learning and of the power of the Church: "it is Cristes conseil that I seye, / And if thou telle it man, thou art forlore" (3504-05). He uses his connection with the other clerks to silence John at the end of the tale: "For every clerk anonright heeld with oother. / They seyde, 'The man is wood, my leeve brother'" (3847-48). So Nicholas is superb at manipulating the social order. And again, as his epithet suggests, *hendeness* in the world-view of the tale is just that—skill at various kinds of manipulation.

With less success, Absalom, too, tries to manipulate various social structures. He woos Alisoun by the book (3371 ff.), but he neglects the appropriate kind of manipulation that Nicholas is expert in. "Somtyme, to shewe his lightnesse and maistrye, / He pleyeth Herodes upon a scaffold hye" (3383-84), using the mystery play for his own advancement in love. He does make a fool of himself by his ineptness in courtly-love language:

> ... for youre love I swete ther I go.
> No wonder is thogh that I swelte and swete;
> I moorne as dooth a lamb after the tete.   (3702-04)

But the point is that it does not much matter what one says, as long as one keeps his attention on the main objective. Absalom's failure to do that is his mistake. He asks for Alisoun's lips when he really wants something else; ironically, he gets what he really wanted, but not as he expected to get it.

Alisoun herself is described in decidedly physical terms (3233 ff.), with multiple similes comparing her to animals and, perhaps more significantly, to all the signs of material prosperity—sheep, cattle, horses, orchards, milk, pear-trees, wool, swallows in a barn, a hoard of apples, sweet drinks, money. Nor is she above manipulating the marriage relationship, that microcosm of the social order, for the satisfaction of her bodily desires:

> And she was war, and knew it bet than he,
> What al this queynte cast was for to seye.
> But nathelees she ferde as she wolde deye,
> And seyde, "Allas! go forth thy wey anon,
> Help us to scape, or we been dede echon!
> I am thy trewe, verray wedded wyf;
> Go, deere spouse, and help to save oure lyf."   (3604-10)

John's uxoriousness, to which Alisoun cold-bloodedly appeals here, might seem to clear him of the charge of living in a world composed only of bodies. Is there not some genuine love of Alisoun as a person, evident in John's reaction to Nicholas' bad news? John thinks first not of himself but of his wife: "This carpenter answerde, 'Allas, my wyf! / And shal she drenche? allas, myn Alisoun!'" (3522-23). But in fact it later appears that John's imagination is rather bodily, too:

> Lo, which a greet thyng is affeccioun!
> Men may dyen of ymaginacioun,
> So depe may impressioun be take.
> This sely carpenter bigynneth quake;
> Hym thynketh verraily that he may see
> Noees flood come walwynge as the see
> To drenchen Alisoun, his hony deere.   (3611-17)

In the world-view of the tale, John's "love" for Alisoun does not clear him of living in a purely material universe; it merely convicts him of "affeccioun"—i.e., folly. And John, too, with less success than most, attempts to use the social institutions of marriage to cater to his own bodily appetites, by restricting Alisoun with a husband's power: "Jalous he was, and heeld hire narwe in cage, / For she was wylde and yong, and he was old" (3224-25).

The entire drama of the misdirected kiss is of course excruciatingly physical. Absalom's itchy mouth (3682), his dream of a feast (3684, recalling the "cat-and-mouse" metaphor at 3346-47), his chewing of breath-freshening herbs, all prepare for the explicit "thyng al rough and long yherd" that Alisoun thrusts out of the window. Nicholas' pun—"A berd! a berd" (3742—"a joke" and "pubic hair")—emphasizes the physicality of fabliau wit, and Absalom's cure is also physical: "Who rubbeth now, who froteth now his lippes / With dust, with sond, with straw, with clooth, with chippes" (3747-48). Absalom has learned his lesson: "Of paramours he sette nat a kers" (3756), where *paramours* is the technical term referring to the courtly-love relationship—there is no suggestion that Absalom will remain celibate forever. He will swallow any insult but the physical (3388, 3708). Now, however, he wishes "Of this despit awroken for to be" (3752). His planned revenge is thoroughly physical. And interestingly enough, Nicholas brings himself in range of the plowshare almost as an afterthought, since he is out of bed anyway: "This Nicholas was risen for to pisse, / And thoughte he wolde amenden all the jape" (3798-99). His joke on the "squaymous" Absalom follows from, and itself consists of, a release of bodily pressure.

Nicholas' climactic cry for "Water!" has a definite empirical meaning for Nicholas, and an entirely different, foolish, fantastical meaning for John. That there are two kinds of water is indicative of the world-view of the tale. The water that might cool Nicholas' "towte" is real—it makes sense to look for it. Indeed, it is urgent that one look for it. The water that

John fears is imaginary, like most of the strictures, ideals, and obligations that motivate the characters in the Knight's tale. Anyone who thinks that kind of water is real is a fool. John *is*, in a deep sense, "wood," as the clerks say, and exactly as Nicholas promised him he would become if he betrayed Nicholas' strategem (3507). The irony is that John is already mad, to believe, like the characters in the Knight's tale, in something that he cannot see.

In the world-view of the Miller's tale, then, man is essentially just a body, and society is just a collection of bodies. Intellect is respected and rewarded only to the extent that it serves bodily desires. John speaks perfectly in the spirit of the tale when he talks about the foolishness of the philosopher who fell in the pit while looking at the stars (3457 ff.). Nicholas' more practical sort of astrology makes better sense. And John is still a fool to be applying his exemplum to Nicholas. Social order in the tale is nothing more than a shifting structure of more or less loose, temporary alliances entered into for mutual benefit or mutual exploitation. And so this world-view must be ultimately unsatisfactory. It is a bracing contrast to the lofty perspective of the Knight's tale, but the world-view of the Miller's tale deconstructs itself. It cannot explain why, if the world is so clearly composed only of bodies, men get so confused about what is real. We know, too, that there are in fact sincere scholars, faithful lovers, chaste marriages, and wise men. There is something in the world besides bodies, something that sometimes can be an even more powerful motivation than bodily desires. And there is some bedrock of lasting value in the multifarious manifestations of the social order. Already, however, by juxtaposing the Knight's world-view with the Miller's, the first fragment suggests that no world-view is going to be adequate that explains human experience in terms of the dialectic between social order and individual freedom.

The Reeve's Tale

The Reeve's tale is perhaps less controversial even than the Miller's. Most read the tale as a fabliau, a dramatic reply to the Miller's attack on carpenters, and most point out that the main difference between the Miller and the Reeve is that the Reeve portrays a world altogether nastier.[29] Especially, critics notice how repellent the Reeve's attitude toward sex is in contrast with the Miller's tale.[30]

The sexual crudity of the Reeve's tale, however, should not be allowed to obscure the essential point of difference between this tale and the Miller's. The world of the Reeve's tale is not a world composed solely of bodies, even though the concrete diction of the Reeve's prologue makes us expect a tale about such a world. We might say that the world of the Miller's tale is amoral, while the world of the Reeve's tale is immoral. Amorality is perhaps the only reasonable stance in a world composed solely of bodies. But in the Reeve's tale there can also be immorality, and for the reason that Alfred David suggests in his acute discussion of sex in the tale: "Sex in the Reeve's Tale is the principal instrument in a savage class satire. The seductions are the means of crushing the pretensions of Symkyn and his wife to be superior to the other peasants."[31] In short, the important thing in the Reeve's tale is not a person's body or his bodily desires, but the position of that person in the social hierarchy. Where we have a society of persons, and not just a collection of bodies, morality and immorality become possible.

The description of Symkyn that opens the tale immediately shows how things are going to go. The epithet in "deynous Symkyn" (3941) invites the obvious comparison with "hende Nicholas," and "deynous" is as important a concept in the Reeve's tale as "hende" is in the preceding tale. Symkyn and his wife are both disdainful, but with no good reason. He is ape-like (3935), somewhat sub-human; she is "smoterlich" (3963). And so the point of Symkyn's weaponry, with which he bristles like a pincushion, and of his reputation as a "market-betere" (3936) is clear: he violently imposes on his fellows a perverted social order. Symkyn's family rises to a social position above themselves because a priest descended beneath himself. What holds the family together, moreover, is not bodily desire or descent, but pride of place:

> For Symkyn wolde no wyf, as he sayde,
> But she were wel ynorissed and a mayde,
> To saven his estaat of yomanrye.   (3947-49)

And when Symkyn attacks Aleyn in the dark, he cries, "Who dorste be so boold to disparage / My doghter, that is come of swich lynage?" (4271-72).

The clerks, too, are less concerned with the loss of wheat or the physical discomfort of chasing horses in the rain, than they are with the intellectual pecking order in which one man has the right to scorn another as a fool:

> "Allas," quod John, "the day that I was born!
> Now are we dryve til hethyng and til scorn.
> Oure corn is stoln, men wil us fooles calle,
> Bathe the wardeyn and oure felawes alle,
> And namely the millere, weylaway!"   (4109-13)

And as John lies "as a draf-sak" in bed, while Aleyn is trying his luck with Maleyne, he says to himself,

> Now may I seyn that I is but an ape.
> . . . .
> And when this jape is tald another day,
> I sal been halde a daf, a cokenay!   (4202-08)

In the Reeve's tale, then, the world is not a world of bodies only, but a world of "oneupsmanship." The point is not so much to satisfy one's body, as to put oneself over someone else. Aleyn says, "yon wenche wil I swyve," because the law allows compensation for injuries done; "And syn I sal have neen amendement / Agayn my los, I will have esement" (4178-86). His concern is not primarily to satisfy his bodily desires; nor is that John's concern later. Sex is aggression and revenge, but it is not purely physical aggression or revenge as Absalom's was. In such a world, bodies are only what makes people vulnerable to other people. Symkyn can cheat the scholars because the scholars have to eat, and his is the only mill in the vicinity. The horse's "'wehee,' thurgh thikke and thurgh thenne" as he chases after the wild mares (4066) is a perfect exemplum of how bodies in the tale lead their possessors on a wild chase, leaving them "Wery and wet, as beest is in the reyn" (4107). Aleyn can get his revenge because of Maleyne's drunkenness and because of her (putative) maidenhead, and John can get his because, in an interesting reversal on the Miller's tale, the wife "wente hire out to pisse" (4215). The brutality of the tale emphasizes what bodies are—they are means of hurting others in order to assert superiority over them: "by the throte-bolle he caughte Alayn" (4273); "And in the floor, with nose and mouth tobroke, / They walwe as doon two pigges in a poke" (4277-78); "Thise clerkes beete hym weel and lete hym lye" (4308).

So the clerks defeat the miller. And yet, they are not a great deal cleverer than he is. Their rising above him in the intellectual pecking order is as much an unjust imposition as Symkyn's own insistence on his family's social status. Aleyn's greatest success comes, in fact, not from planning but from acting on impulse. John urges prudence (4188), but Aleyn says only, "I counte hym nat a flye" (4192). John admires, not Aleyn's intellect, but his recklessness: "He auntred hym, and has his nedes sped" (4205). And here we come to perhaps the most interesting comparison between the Miller's tale and the Reeve's tale. In both tales, as Owen points out, the character who is ultimately duped by clerks makes a disparaging comment on learning.[32] John's comment is the story of the clerk who fell into the pit (3457-61). And when Symkyn

43

thinks he has a secure upper hand, and the clerks are reduced to begging him for dinner and lodging, he twits them unmercifully:

> Myn hous is streit, but ye han lerned art;
> Ye konne by argumentes make a place
> A myle brood of twenty foot of space.
> Lat se now if this place may suffise,
> Or make it rowm with speche, as is your gise.   (4122-26)

Symkyn seems to be suggesting, among other things, that the contest is over. The clerks can hardly expect to get away with anything in such close quarters, with the bully Symkyn threateningly at hand. In fact, however, the clerks do succeed in making "room" for their revenge—not, indeed, by means of argument and speech, just as Nicholas does not fool John by means of his knowledge of astrology. Symkyn's small chamber can expand to any size required for the clerks' game of oneupsmanship.

Darkness and confusion are crucial to the plot in the Reeve's tale, and they are also crucial in the Miller's tale. But the Miller's tale is dependent on spatial relationships in a way that the Reeve's tale is not. The difference between *inside* the bower and *outside*, between *up* in the roof and *down* on the floor, is of essence in the Miller's tale.[33] The shot-window, so meticulously placed, is essential. To play their jokes on Absalom, Alisoun and Nicholas must thrust themselves out the window. To get his revenge, Absalom must locate his target precisely: "Spek, sweete bryd, I noot nat where thou art" (3805). And the climactic movement in the "Noah's-flood" plot is John's sudden precipitation: "doun gooth al; he foond neither to selle, / Ne breed ne ale, til he cam to the celle / Upon the floor" (3821-23). Spatial relationships are a kind of absolute in the Miller's tale. Bodies exist in space and are dependent upon spatial relationships. Spatial relationships are the "given" upon which the various transient social orders are constructed—manipulation of social orders means bodily movement in an absolute space.

In the Reeve's tale, however, the spatial relationships themselves are easily manipulated in the dark. Aleyn has no trouble sneaking to Maleyne's bed. If John wants to make the wife confuse his bed with Symkyn's, he just moves the cradle—thus in an important sense *making* his bed Symkyn's bed, both for the wife and later for Aleyn. The crucial thing is not how things are located in space, but how they appear to the characters. The miller's wife "knew the estres bet than dide this John," and so she quickly finds a staff. But when it comes to using it, she has trouble locating her target:

44

And by that light she saugh hem bothe two,
But sikerly she nyste who was who,
But as she saugh a whit thyng in hir ye.   (4299-301)

Unfortunately for Symkyn, the "whit thyng" is his "pyled skulle"; and so, like John in the Miller's tale, "doun he gooth" (4306-07). Social relationships in the Reeve's tale are not crucially dependent on spatial relationships. The important thing is not the spatial coordinates of things, but what signification the human perceiver places on the spatial relationships perceived. Thus, a tiny dark room might as well be a mile broad, for the purposes of the Reeve's tale.

The world-view that the Reeve's tale shows us, then, is unsatisfactory because in this view life is thoroughly nasty, crude, and brutal. In terms of the ongoing dialectic begun by the Knight's tale and continued in the Miller's tale, the Reeve offers a third, less attractive way of looking at things. The Reeve's tale shows that individual freedom is restricted, and human intellect corrupted, by the unjust imposition of perverted social hierarchies that are, nevertheless, the most important thing to human beings. Even our bodily life, the tale seems to show, is secondary to our concern for getting ahead of someone else in some hierarchy. Our bodies are only that which makes us vulnerable to the brutal, all-out game of oneupsmanship that is the essence of human life. For the Reeve, sex exists only in the service of self-aggrandizement. And the Knight's attempt to portray a universal order is more deeply deluded, given what social order really is. Theseus, in the world-view of the Reeve's tale, is really no better than Symkyn. And on this depressing note, Chaucer begins the Cook's fragment.

The Cook's Tale

As I suggested earlier, several critics have seen the incomplete Cook's tale as the last convulsion in the degenerative movement obvious in fragment I.[34] The Cook's tale also serves to destroy the dialectic set up in the preceding three tales by reducing it to meaninglessness. Perkyn's life is neither free in any meaningful sense nor ordered. He merely performs random motion. He will "love" anybody (4372-74): "Wel was the wenche with hym myghte meete" (whoever she is). He is a drinker (4376) and a waster: "he was free / Of his dispense" (4387-88). Perkyn's freedom here is license, and his expenditures on "dys, riot, or paramour" (4392) should be compared to Theseus' vast but not wasteful expenditures on the stadium and the temples—expenditures in the interest of creating social order. Perkyn is also a thief and a liar: "Revel and trouthe, as in a lowe degree, / They been ful wrothe al day, as men may

45

see" (4397-98). We see in the fragmentary tale the breakdown of the commercial relation between master and apprentice, a time-honored social structure for getting the work of the world done. We also see the breakdown of the microcosm of all social order, the marriage relationship. The wife of Perkyn's friend "heeld for contenance / A shoppe, and swyved for hir sustenance" (4421-22). Even in the bleak view of the Reeve's tale, the family unit held together—not through love, certainly, but through pride in social caste; and when Maleyne in a moment of weakness betrays Symkyn, it is not just through "swyvyng," but because of some deluded feeling.

In short, the Cook's fragment shows us human beings as utterly careless—careless about their goods, about other people, and about themselves. In such a world-view, social order is of course impossible, and the question of human freedom is meaningless. With the Cook's tale we reach a destination implicit in fragment I from its beginning. That destination is the conclusion that human life cannot be adequately understood in terms of the categories of social order and human freedom. Either those categories are irreconcilable, or else the one taken to be the primary category fails adequately to subsume the other. Finally, as happens in the Cook's tale, we can postulate a "realistic" human situation where *neither* of the categories seems to mean much. Thus, we end fragment I with a sense of dissatisfaction much deeper than can be accounted for by our experience of any individual tale, or of the incompletenessss of the final tale. A whole approach to the explanation of human life has failed, has proven itself inadequate to reconcile in a satisfactory way the world-views that may possibly arise from that approach. We need a new approach, a new set of categories.

CHAPTER FOUR

Fragment II:
The Christian Categories

The Man of Law's Tale

The Man of Law's tale presents us with a new set of categories. The attempts to understand the human condition in terms of the dialectic between social order and human freedom have failed. In the world-view implicit in the Man of Law's tale, social order is of little importance, and human freedom can be understood only in the larger context of God's providence. The tale looks at many of the same themes as the first fragment—Fortune, love, sovereignty, marriage, treachery, revenge, intellect—but these themes are seen from a radically different perspective. We could not have understood Perkyn as a member of the social order or as a responsible free agent, but we can certainly understand him as a sinner.

Several critics have pointed out the various ways in which the Man of Law's tale serves as a contrast or as a complement to the Knight's tale.[1] Carol V. Kaske shows that an obvious difference between the two tales appears in their respective analyses of causation, of the ideas of Fortune, destiny, and Providence; Kaske notes that the causes of misfortune in the Knight's tale are Boethian—Fortune, "aventure," "cas"—whereas in the Man of Law's tale there are specifically Christian causes—miraculous interventions.[2] The Man of Law's tale explains why a consideration of social orders, as products of human wisdom, can never completely account for the human condition. There is an important difference between the characters of the Knight's tale and Constance. Palamon, Arcite, and especially Theseus are struggling to arrive with their human wisdom at an understanding and acceptance of their condition. Constance is not. As Ruggiers says, the Man of Law's tale exhibits "a thoroughly Christian point of view in which the will has not had to be corrected or shaped or molded, but is correctly oriented toward the Deity from the outset in a wholly salutary trust."[3]

But of course the new point of view in the Man of Law's tale has always been gravely problematic for critics. There is a deep tension in the tale between the undeniably Christian message and our emotional

responses to Constance's sufferings. As theodicy, the tale has question-
able success. It is interesting that both Trevor Whittock[4] and Alfred
David[5] focus on the Host's words in the introduction as important for
an understanding of the tale. Whittock reads the Host's words (16 ff.) as
"calling for something beyond this unsatisfactory and imperfect world"
of the first fragment; the Man of Law responds with a "moral allegory"
(p. 108). But David rather focusses on the "gloomy impression of
mutability" that is stronger in the Man of Law's tale even than in the
Knight's tale, in spite of the "Christian context" of the Man of Law's
tale (pp. 128-29). The Host is talking about how time gets away from us.
If his speech has any sincere undertones at all, and is not just another of
the verbal improvisations he likes so much, then it seems a bit strange,
coming from the man whose suggestion it was "to shorte with oure
weye" (General Prologue, 791) by telling tales. The Host is saying in the
Man of Law's introduction, oddly, that the pilgrims must hurry to tell
the tales whose function is to pass the time. The speech quite clearly
introduces the issue of the use of time, no matter how seriously we take
the Host's words. Contrasted with his earlier words about the plan for
the pilgrimage, the speech calls into question the value of human
activity. If what we are doing is just "passing time," in the first place,
does it make any sense to worry about idleness? Or, in more abstract
terms, if human action has no significance in itself, why should we
experience the *care* that Heidegger tells us is the fundamental character
of being in the world? What is the use of time, the point of human life in
time? This question is at the heart of the tension in the Man of Law's
tale. The world-view shown in the tale is ultimately unsatisfactory
because it allows so little significance to human action, so little value to
human experience. What Constance does or suffers ultimately does not
seem to matter, since she has little control over her fate and is already
perfect. Thus, the Man of Law's tale in answering the degenerative
movement of the first fragment falls into error on the other side, an error
that goads into action the Wife of Bath and the pilgrims who follow in
her train.

Various critics have identified the tension at the heart of the Man of
Law's tale in various ways, and have accounted for it or explained it
away in various ways, both on dramatic and on thematic grounds.[6] But
most have felt the need to reconcile what Eugene Clasby calls the "two
perspectives on the narrative: the temporal and the eternal."[7] Certainly from the eternal perspective Constance seems completely in God's
hands. Whatever happens to her is attributed directly to God—it is
"Goddes sonde," a theme sounded again and again in the tale (see, for
example, lines 283-84, 511, 523, 538, 566-71, 686, 693, 760, 825-26, 902,

945, 1041-43, and 1160-61). Even when Constance's physical wrestling with her would-be rapist causes him to fall into the sea, the event is attributed to Christ: "And thus hath Crist unwemmed kept Custance" (924). From the temporal perspective, however, we see a considerably less secure and less intelligible world. The reiterative story, with its two evil mothers-in-law, its lustful knight and heathen rapist, its reappearances of Satan as adversary, shows us the opposite of what the Knight's tale shows. In both, the imposition of earthly order is doomed, but in the Knight's tale it is important strenuously to seek the earthly order that corresponds with the universal order. The Man of Law's tale shows that all earthly orders are pretty much alike, and all are vain and transitory. Indeed, no sooner are Constance's problems solved, and no sooner is she settled with her husband Alla in England, than Alla dies, and the settlement toward which the narrative has been tending is dispelled. Seeking social order is like building sandcastles before the tide. The Knight's "Firste Moevere" becomes the Man of Law's "O firste moevyng! crueel firmament!" (295). Man's perception is also clouded. The wisdom that might permit him to see how to live is lacking. God's will is written in the stars (190-96), but "we been to lewed or to slowe" (315) to read it. [8]

Constance herself from the temporal perspective (the perspective, to be sure, of many modern readers of Chaucer), though perfectly in harmony with God's will, seems characterized by what some critics call "passivity" and what some call "detachment." In any case, her character is bothersome. Clasby attempts to answer this objection by arguing that the question is not whether Constance is virtuous, but "whether that virtue will be recognized for what it is and whether she will be able to maintain . . . a vision of herself as virtuous and innocent. . . ."[9] Thus, the suffering is not meaningless, but Constance grows and is strengthened by her experience (pp. 232, 225). My own reading of the tale would emphasize instead the circular, non-progressive character of Constance's experience. After Alla dies, she returns to the home she left so reluctantly and with such lamenting (260 ff.). It is as though the intervening years and experiences have been wiped away, forgotten like a bad dream:

> To Rome is come this hooly creature,
> And fyndeth hire freendes hoole and sounde;
> Now is she scaped al hire aventure.
> And whan that she hir fader hath yfounde,
> Doun on hir knees falleth she to grounde;
> Wepynge for tendrenesse in herte blithe,
> She heryeth God an hundred thousand sithe. (1149-55)

What most of us might call a life, and a hard one at that, for Constance has been merely an "aventure" (note the echo of the important word from the Knight's tale) from which she has returned. The death of the Sultan, her love for Alla and their loss and reunion seem to have gone out of her mind, and she is back to precisely where she was and precisely what she was when the story began. Of course, we should no doubt read the passage I have quoted as suggesting also the Christian's entry into heaven when the tears of this life will be wiped away. But that is just the point. If we regard human experience that way, as a bad dream that passes away, what is the significance of that dream as we live it? What, to return to the words of the Host, is the use of time?

Nowhere is the problem more clearly focussed in the tale than in a passage which reads almost as if it is calculated especially to sting the Wife of Bath, of all the pilgrims, into a reply—namely, the Man of Law's discussion of Constance's sex-life:

> They goon to bedde, as it was skile and right;
> For thogh that wyves be ful hooly thynges,
> They moste take in pacience at nyght
> Swiche manere necessaries as been plesynges
> To folk that han ywedded hem with rynges,
> And leye a lite hir hoolynesse aside,
> As for the tyme,—it may no bet bitide.   (708-14)

The apparent delicacy of this passage, unsuccessfully attempting to mask its crudity,[10] shows how the world-view of the tale falls short. The tale has little to say about sex as a bodily function, and nothing to say about sex in marriage as an emblem of lawful earthly pleasure or an expression of human love. The world-view of the tale calls into serious question the value and significance of earthly experience. The treatment of sexual experience in marriage is here only symptomatic of the general inability to give experience its due, but of course it is a symptom appearing in an area where the Wife of Bath is "expert." And so the Man of Law's tale prepares us for her performance and the performances of the rest of the pilgrims who follow along in the so-called "Marriage Group."

CHAPTER FIVE

Fragments III-IV-V:
The Value of Earthly Experience

Critics have debated about the "Marriage Group" since Kittredge. Some have denied that any debate among the pilgrims exists;[1] some have added to[2] or subtracted from[3] the four tales traditionally placed in the group. Obviously the question about whether there is a debate is a question about whether to read the group dramatically, since nobody denies that the four tales traditionally placed in the group treat marriage as a theme. As R. E. Kaske has shown,[4] the themes of sex and *maistrie* in marriage are the themes important for the reading of the group as a debate. But other themes are as prominent. There is, for example, the theme of *gentilesse*.[5] We have the hag's sermon on the theme in the Wife's tale, the dialogue in the Clerk's tale between Walter's nobility and Griselda's low birth, January's perversion of *gentilesse* in the Merchant's tale, and the Franklin's definition of *gentilesse* in his tale. *Trouthe* is also a theme. In the Wife's tale, the knight plights his *trouthe* to the hag. Griselda faithfully keeps her promise to Walter under impossible conditions, whereas May is a quick-witted, conscienceless liar who cheerfully breaks her marriage vows. And in the Franklin's tale, of course, "Trouthe is the hyeste thyng that man may kepe" (V.1479).

All of these tales also question the uses and the power of the human intellect, sometimes in ways reminiscent of the tales in fragment I. The hag wins ascendancy over the knight by power of intellect. Walter's testing of Griselda appears, even to the narrator, as a kind of perversion of intellect, a desire to know too much and to inquire too deeply into another human being's soul. Trust, faith, and endurance seem more important here than intellect. In the Merchant's tale, January's physical blindness is the analogue of his intellectual blindness, as the "debate" between Justinus and Placebo highlights. And in the Franklin's tale, evil seems to take the form of *illusion*—Dorigen's intellectual confusion, the clerk's magic.

Finally, all four tales deal in interestingly different ways with the theme of the use of worldly goods. The hag's sermon points out that poverty is a good, in an ironic contrast to the "thing-oriented" Wife. The Clerk seems to despise worldly goods except as symbols of spiritual things, as the carefully worked-out symbolism of Griselda's clothing suggests. January tries to buy love—or at least sex—with his possessions; for him money is power, the potential for aggression, both civil and sexual. And in the Franklin's tale, wealth is the unstated basis of the *fre* way of life, the life of upperclass leisure his characters live. When one has money, one does not have to think about it—consider Aurelius' indifference to the thousand pounds. Money is merely a way of supporting or demonstrating a higher good, magnanimity of character.

Besides these common themes, which can certainly be related to the question of marriage but are by no means exhausted by the supposed debate on sex and *maistrie*, there has always been another embarrassment in reading the Marriage Group dramatically. The Friar's tale, the Summoner's tale, and the Squire's tale appear as "interludes," motivated, to be sure, by dramatic interactions, but not clearly related to the marriage debate. Critics who read thematically often attempt to address this problem by suggesting that marriage in *The Canterbury Tales* is not *just* marriage, but instead is emblematic of something more. Specifically, marriage is taken to represent "a well-ordered hierarchy of almost any kind,"[6] the institution through which "mankind achieves its fullest expression and perfection in the natural order."[7] Critics who see marriage in *The Canterbury Tales* this way want to extend the discussion of marriage far beyond the tales of fragments III-V; and as D. W. Robertson, Jr., points out, once we see that Chaucer's treatment of marriage is "thematic rather than dramatic, the false problems raised by the old theory of the 'marriage group' disappear."[8]

Following this hint, then, I want to argue that a thematic reading of *The Canterbury Tales* finds in fragments III-V not a debate on marriage, but a series of tales about the value and significance of earthly experience in general. The Man of Law's tale prepares us for such a series—and especially, for the Wife's initiation of it—by its implication that human action (particularly, sexual action) is insignificant. The Wife's tale and its followers try to restore the balance, to give earthly experience its due. In this reading, marriage becomes simply the representative human action. It is representative, not only because marriage is a type in the medieval mind, but also because most human beings experience their deepest feelings and their greatest extremes of emotion—from euphoria to despair—as a consequence of the marriage relationship. The Knight's tale defines the two most important earthly activities as love and war; the Wife's prologue points out that marriage includes both. A marriage, then, as the smallest social unit, serves as a microcosm of man's earthly condition, the exemplary earthly experience.[9]

There is some justification for regarding the Wife's prologue as a tale in its own right, and certainly the performance there is more striking than her tale itself. But I shall, on principle, pass over the frame-story, while admitting that any reading of the Wife's tale that divorces it from the context of her prologue is a partial reading.

Most of the critics who argue that it is appropriate for the Wife to follow the Man of Law argue on the basis of her prologue.[10] But Lee S. Cox also points out strong contrasts between the Man of Law's performance and the Wife's *tale*: the hag's sermon on poverty satirizes the Man of Law's attitude toward wealth; and the Wife "implies that earthly authority can deal with the crime" of rape (if the woman has sovereignty), whereas the Man of Law "invokes divine authority and judgment for rapists."[11]

Once we begin contrasting the rapists in the two tales, it is easy to take the scene in the Wife's tale as an ironic inversion of the scene in the tale of Constance. In both tales, the narrative of the actual rape or attempted rape is mercilessly bare and quick. In the Man of Law's tale, the steward comes onto the ship in line 916 and is thrown overboard in line 922; in the Wife's tale, the knight has seen the maiden and completed the rape in the space of three lines. But in the Man of Law's tale, the story follows the fate of the victim, and the criminal literally drops out of sight. It is the other way around in the Wife's tale—no one seems particularly interested in the further doings of the maiden.[12] But the crucial point is this: the brief narrative in the Man of Law's tale is expanded for three stanzas with apostrophes and moralizations: "O foule lust of luxurie, lo, thyn ende!" (925), "How may this wayke womman han this strengthe . . . ?" (932), "Who yaf Judith corage or hardynesse . . . ?" (939). The narrator tells us at length what the lesson of the rape is, thus underscoring that Constance herself, the near-victim, learns nothing from it. She has nothing to learn. She remains just as she was before, and indeed, that changeless perfection is the problem with Constance seen as a human being. The whole point of the Wife's tale, however, is that the knight eventually learns something from his experience. We get no long discussion of the immorality of rape, beyond the passing remark that beheading was the punishment: "Paraventure swich was the statut tho" (893). But what the tale does not say, it shows. It shows that earthly experience can be significant, can teach us something. That thesis is what the world-view of the Man of Law's tale seemed consistently to deny in attributing all earthly events to an inscrutable Providence.

From the early lines of the Wife's tale it is clear that the point is for the knight to learn something. The queen tells him, "I yeve thee leve for to gon / A twelf-month and a day, to seche and leere" (908-09). The suggestion is that God works through human experience to teach his creatures—the knight is to return "With swich answere as God wolde hym purveye" (917). When he sees the ladies dancing, the knight draws nearer "In hope that som wysdom sholde he lerne" (994), and the hag speaks of *teaching* him something. The reader himself is involved in this attempt to learn from experience. Not only does the reader follow the knight in his quest for the answer to that impossible question, but also the reader is sent to find out things on his own. The Wife most curiously breaks off the tale of Midas' ears just before its dénouement, destroying the effectiveness of Ovid's story and making her own point less forcefully than she might, with the following advice: "The remenant of the tale if ye wol heere, / Redeth Ovyde, and ther ye may it leere" (981-82).

If the reader were as thick-witted as the knight, he would have a difficult time learning anything at all, and a difficult time understanding the tale. The knight's good looks, not his intellect, seem to be his strong point. He has no answer when the queen asks her riddle, and the trouble with relying for an answer on authority, the traditional alternative to experience, is that authorities disagree:

> But he ne koude arryven in no coost
> Wher as he myghte fynde in this mateere
> Two creatures accordynge in-feere.   (922-24)

The most intelligent decision the knight makes, of course, is to leave the thinking to someone else.[13]

The hag demonstrates the power of her intellect not only in her answer to the queen's riddle, but also in the "sermon" she delivers to her new husband when he explains his lack of sexual eagerness. This sermon has always been somewhat problematic in interpretations of the tale, and often it has been accounted for on dramatic grounds, by arguing that it is meant to tell us something about the Wife of Bath herself.[14] But the sermon is scarcely what it purports to be. It purports to be an argument to show that low birth, poverty, old age, and ugliness should not be barriers to love. In fact, however, the section of the sermon that deals with *gentilesse* is a thinly disguised rebuke to the knight for his "ungentle" deeds: "For, God it woot, men may wel often fynde / A lordes sone do shame and vileynye" (1150-51); "He nys nat gentil, be he duc or erl; / For vileyns synful dedes make a cherl" (1157-58). The hag then strikes closer to home, with a change of pronoun that is personal in more than the grammatical sense:

> For gentillesse nys but renomee
> Of thyne auncestres, for hire heigh bountee,
> Which is a strange thyng to thy persone.   (1159-61)

Certainly the argument is correct, but rebuking one's husband for past misdeeds is hardly the way to remove a barrier to love. The section of the sermon dealing with poverty "proves" only that Christ lived in poverty and that a poor man is better off than a rich man because he has fewer worries and knows himself better. Again, the doctrine is good (and applies backhandedly to the knight's lack of self-knowledge), but it is hardly an argument that the poor person is worthy of romantic love. The principle that "men sholde an oold wight doon favour, / And clepe hym fader" (1210-11) certainly does nothing to induce sexual desire for old women; and the observation that "filthe and eelde" are "grete wardeyns upon chastitee" (1215-16) is actually a reason for the young knight's squeamishness. So the doctrine does not jibe with the ostensible purpose of the sermon. And if we are to be in on the joke, we must understand, and believe that the hag understands, the absurdity of producing reasons like these to "prove" that she is lovable. What is affirmed here is not the doctrine, but the natural human feeling of the knight that he would rather have a sexually desirable wife.

And of course, the hag in her wisdom, after she has played with the knight and amused the reader, herself affirms the value of the knight's human feeling: "But nathelees, syn I knowe your delit, / I shal fulfille youre worldly appetit" (1217-18). When the knight is wise enough to give her her way, she becomes both fair and young, affirming the value of young love and human sexual experience. Thus, on a deep level, the world-view of the Wife's tale "answers" the world-view of the tale of Constance, where human experience seems to be only a pale, uninteresting shadow of an inscrutable divine purpose.

The Friar's Tale

P. R. Szittya has treated thoroughly the numerous parallels between the Wife's tale and the Friar's tale.[15] Besides the dramatic interaction between the two pilgrims, there are various thematic contrasts between the tales—different conceptions of *trouthe*, different sorts of "teaching" (pp. 389-90). And the Friar parodies the Wife's assertion of experience over authority, when in lines 1515-22 and 1636-38 the yeoman suggests that the summoner will become an authority on devils through his actual experience (p. 391). If Szittya's listing of verbal and thematic parallels were not already enough to show that the Friar's tale is an answer of some sort to the Wife's, the lines in question ought to do so. For the rather odd image in line 1518, where the summoner "Konne in a chayer rede of this sentence," has as its source the very passage in the *Romance of the Rose* (lines 12815-17, the speech of La Vielle) that is also the source for the beginning of the Wife's prologue. Thus, the Wife's prologue and the Friar's tale seem to be linked by the theme of human experience, the theme I have identified as the controlling theme of fragments III-V.

For me, Szittya's most interesting remark is that the Friar's tale parodies the Wife's because it is "meant to demonstrate to us how utterly out of place her notions of reality are in what the Friar sees as the real world" (p. 390). In other words, the difference in the two tales is a difference in the world-views implicit in them. The Friar's tale exhibits dissatisfaction with the "niceness" of the Wife's tale. Szittya thus agrees with what everyone has always said about the Wife's tale—namely, that it is at heart a fairy tale; and while a fairy tale can be a charming story or even inculcate a moral, things just do not happen that way in the "real world."

It is perhaps not so easy to see how the Friar's tale extends the theme of the group, the idea that human experience is valuable and significant. The great critical problem in the Friar's tale has always been to explain the summoner's behavior. Why does he stay with the yeoman, and indeed reaffirm his oath of brotherhood, in the face of the most explicit warnings? Most critics of the tale have addressed this problem. Some explain the summoner's behavior simply by accusing him of stupidity or obtuseness.[16] D. W. Robertson, Jr., on the other hand, accounts for the lack of psychological realism by making the summoner a "concrete manifestation of a moral concept," namely the "insatiable curiosity . . . in *visibilia*," accompanied by an inability to understand *invisibilia* "even when they are patiently and authoritatively explained to him."[17] Other critics see the summoner as caught by his own deviousness—he does not believe the devil, because he himself, in the devil's place, would have been lying.[18] Still others see the summoner's unconcern as following naturally from his complete commitment to evil—it is too late for him to choose good, at this point.[19]

I think, however, that Szittya's comment is again most illuminating. He says that the summoner "either doesn't care or doesn't believe what he is told" (p. 390). The insight that the summoner might be *careless* in a deep sense is, I think, a very important one. As I have noted before, the fundamental character of being in the world, in Heidegger's terminology, is care. To be *careless*, then, is to fail to be in the world properly, to fail to grapple responsibly with one's existential situation. Without trying to make an existentialist out of Chaucer (though the notion is not completely silly), I think it is possible to argue that precisely that failure to confront one's existential dilemma is the summoner's problem. The concept of *intent* is crucially important in the tale.[20] Carelessness is the failure to consider intent carefully—both others' intent and, more important, one's own. The summoner is careless in this sense:

> In daliaunce they ryden forth and pleye.
> This somonour, which that was as ful of jangles,
> As ful of venym been thise waryangles,
> And evere enqueryng upon every thing.   (1406-09)

The summoner is always ready to *play*, to talk or dispute idly; he has curiosity without thoughtfulness. And it is precisely at this vulnerable point that the yeoman-devil strikes, approaching him playfully, carelessly as a chance-met fellow. Paul Ruggiers has remarked that our reaction to the tale is controlled by the deliberate coupling of the "inexorable closing in of divine justice" with the "speciously genial in the relationship of demon to victim."[21] Rather than trying to "explain" the summoner's behavior, I think we should recognize a deep and marvelous ambiguity in it, corresponding to the ambiguity in our own reaction to the tale. For the reader this ambiguity runs throughout the tale like an intolerable itch, too deep to get at. And the ambiguity is a response to the summoner's carelessness, considered not as a character-trait that accounts for behavior, but as a fundamental wrongness in his meshing with the world, a superficiality in confronting matters which are important if anything about human life is important. Our irritation is literally our irritation at *not* being able to understand how a human being could exist in the world with his kind of carelessness.

When we say that we do not understand the summoner's carelessness, we imply that in the world-view of the tale human experience is of great value and significance. It is, in other words, worthy of care. The Friar's tale answers the Wife's by showing that human beings will not pay attention to experience. They are perverse in their carelessness. But the Friar's tale also answers the Man of Law's, by showing that experience is worth paying attention to. The summoner's own experience has enormous significance for him, even if his carelessness prevents his understanding it until too late. When the yeoman-devil affirms the value of experience, in the passage most clearly linking this tale to the Wife, he is explicitly warning the summoner of his fiendish intention to provide other-worldly experiences. But he is implicitly warning him to pay attention to, to be changed by, his earthly experiences:

> For thou shalt, by thyn owene experience,
> Konne in a chayer rede of this sentence
> Bet than Virgile.... (1517-19)

Precisely because earthly experience is valuable and significant, gambling playfully with ultimates as the summoner does is surely to lose one's soul.

The Summoner's Tale

If my reading of the Friar's tale seems odd in insisting that the summoner in that tale is unintelligible, I think the reading is nevertheless supported by the next tale, which serves as a kind of gloss on the Friar's tale. In the Summoner's tale, the most obvious critical difficulty concerns the portion that extends from Thomas' "gift-giving" to the end. The simple demands of the fabliau-form are well and truly met as soon as Thomas farts in John's hand, and it has been a matter of controversy to determine the function of the remainder of the tale. Various dramatic solutions have been proposed,[22] including those of several critics who base their conclusions on the medieval iconography of the Apostles at Pentecost.[23] These critics think Jankyn's proposal for parting the fart is a deliberate blasphemous parody designed to deflate the pretensions of friars, who in Chaucer's time often insisted like John that they were the direct spiritual heirs of the Apostles. The "great wind" that visited the Apostles at Pentecost has become a fart for the corrupt friars. Thus, the function of the last part of the tale is to extend its meaning from the crude fabliau-motif into sophisticated antifraternal satire.

W. G. East reads fragment III as a debate on the question of *experience* versus *auctoritee*, and he naturally offers a solution that is a bit closer to my own reading. East points out that Friar John's long-winded, hypocritical sermon, packed full of *auctoritees*, gets in return a question from Thomas that seems impossible to answer by means of *auctoritee*—how can a fart be divided in twelve? But Jankyn "solves the problem 'By preeve which that is demonstratif'—his method is practical, if not practicable."[24] The emphasis on the value of empirical demonstration is already a strong indication of how this tale might fit thematically with the other tales in fragments III-V. As in the Wife's tale and Friar's tale, we have a long passage of ineffective instruction—in this case, Friar John's sermon about the evils of wrath—followed by some definitive experience. Here, though, the one who is delivering the instruction is the one who should be paying attention to it. As Robertson notes, all of Friar John's exempla illustrate the dangers of associating with a wrathful man who has power—but that is what Friar John himself is doing.[25] An

58

explicit mention of *experience* in Friar John's sermon comes in one of these exempla. Cambises tells the courtier who has rebuked him for drunkenness,

> The revers shaltou se...anon,
> And preve it by thyn owene experience,
> That wyn ne dooth to folk no swich offence.   (2056-58)

The threat in line 2057 echos the yeoman-devil's warning to the summoner in the Friar's tale. But the immediate point is that Friar John is doing exactly what he criticizes the courtier for doing—rebuking an angry man for his flaws.

I also feel the normal impulse of the critic to explain away the apparent irrelevance of the last section of the Summoner's tale. But I should prefer to explain the section as a curious sort of gloss on the Friar's tale. Friar John accuses Thomas of blaspheming his convent (2213-15), in a speech that not only reveals his own hypocrisy, but ironically calls attention to Friar John's own blasphemy—his display of contempt for what should be revered.[26] In one sense, Friar John's blasphemy is like the carelessness exhibited by the Friar's summoner. That is, both men fail to show the proper care, the proper reverence, for ultimate matters. But in an important sense, blasphemy is different from carelessness. Blasphemy, or the hypocrisy that is the particular form it takes in Friar John, knows that it blasphemes. It is not "careless"; it takes thought.

The Summoner's tale suggests this difference with two emphatic rhymes early in the tale, both of which call attention to the word *entente*, a word extremely important in the Friar's tale, as we have seen:

> And whan this frere had seyd all his entente,
> With *qui cum patre* forth his wey he wente.   (1733-34)

> To yelden Jhesu Crist his propre rente;
> To sprede his word is set al myn entente.   (1821-22)

Unlike the Friar's summoner, Friar John considers his *entente* carefully. The *entente/wente* rhyme is suggestive once one notices the emphasis in the early lines of the tale on how the friar is always *going* somewhere to get money or other offerings—lines 1736, 1738, 1754, 1765. When he has what he wants, he moves on. The rhyme on *rente/entente* is more obvious—the hypocritical friar attempts subliminally to identify the money he gets with the *rente* due to Christ.

But at the end of the Summoner's tale, the issue is not Friar John's blasphemy, but instead Thomas', an ironic repetition, on a grosser level, of Friar John's irreverence. The focus suddenly shifts from the insult received by Friar John to the puzzle of how Thomas was able to propose such a subtle question. Two explanations are offered. First, there is the lady's:

> I seye, a cherl hath doon a cherles dede.
> What shold I seye? God lat hym nevere thee!
> His sike heed is ful of vanytee:
> I holde hym in a manere frenesye.   (2206-09)

The lord, who is apparently struck more forcibly than his lady, has a different explanation:

> How hadde this cherl ymaginacioun
> To shewe swich a probleme to the frere?
> Nevere erst er now herde I of swich mateere.
> I trow the devel putte it in his mynde.   (2218-21)

> What, lo, my cherl, lo, yet how shrewedly
> Unto my confessour to-day he spak!
> I holde hym certeyn a demonyak!   (2238-40)

In either case, the churl's action is beyond the powers of human comprehension or explanation. There is nothing to do but "ete youre mete, and lat the cherl go pleye" (2241). But the lord's state of mind is now precisely the same state of mind with which the reader contemplates the summoner in the Friar's tale. The summoner's behavior is incomprehensible to us, a mystery and an irritation. The two "solutions" offered to account for Thomas' behavior, interestingly enough, correspond exactly with two of the "solutions" that modern critics have offered to account for the summoner's behavior in the preceding tale. Thomas is either a fool, a churl whose head is full of vanity because of his illness (the lady's solution), or he is completely possessed by evil, a demoniac (the lord's solution)—just as the summoner in the preceding tale has been said to be either intellectually obtuse, or else already completely committed to evil.

The Summoner's tale, then, cannot come to rest, anymore than we can come to rest in our understanding of the summoner in the Friar's tale, unless some other solution is proposed. The Summoner's tale comments on the world-view of the Friar's tale by offering Jankyn's solution. There *is* a way, an empirical, demonstrable way, of answering Thomas, and so the lord and lady need not be bothered by an indissoluble mystery:

> Touchynge the cherl, they seyde, subtiltee
> And heigh wit made hym speken as he spak;
> He nys no fool, ne no demonyak.   (2290-92)

In other words, Thomas' behavior can be analyzed in comprehensible human categories. He is neither irrational nor possessed—he is merely clever, and everyone can rest comfortably in that explanation except Friar John. No one questions whether Thomas in fact had something like Jankyn's solution in mind. The intelligibility of the solution itself guarantees that Thomas is intelligible, that he is not "an inpossible," either.

The Summoner's tale shows us, particularly in the last part, that we can understand evil without invoking the categories of the irrational and the demonic. Simple human hypocrisy, well understood by everyone, and the perversion of the intellect by wrath are sufficient to account for the evil in the Summoner's tale. Perhaps on the dramatic level the Summoner is suggesting that the Friar can easily be dissected, pegged out, and exhausted in terms of common, ordinary categories, and is therefore an altogether less interesting sinner than the summoner in the Friar's own tale. As Friar John says, "Glosynge is a glorious thyng, certeyn" (1793). The last portion of the Summoner's tale seems to take as a main part of its function to "gloss" the Friar's tale and its view of the experience of evil.

The Clerk's Tale

The Clerk most immediately answers the Summoner, by telling a tale about *patience*, the virtue opposed to the sin of wrath dealt with so fully in the Summoner's tale. If the Summoner's tale is about the potential of experience for evil and the perversion of the intellect by wrath, the Clerk's tale is about how patience can turn apparently evil experience into good. But more obvious and more important is the fact that the Clerk answers the Wife, and looks beyond her to the Man of Law's tale. The tale of Griselda has much in common with the tale of Constance, and the Clerk's tale is as much a criticism of the Man of Law's world-view as the Wife's tale is—indeed, perhaps a more valid criticism, philosophically speaking.

Several critics point out that Chaucer does much more in the Clerk's tale than to continue the "debate" on marriage.[27] Many take their cue from the Clerk's own moralization of his tale and read the story typologically, where Griselda's relation to Walter represents the soul's relation to God.[28] But if I were to try to decide what "sophyme" the Clerk is thinking about when the Host first addresses him (line 5),[29] I would say that he had been pondering, not the Wife's view of marriage, but instead the Wife's method of answering the Man of Law's tale. I imagine the Clerk's asking himself how philosophically sound an answer the Wife gave, and how he himself might better answer the tale of Constance. Obviously, there are distortions in the Wife's response. Her tale, triggered by the devaluing of sexual experience in the tale of Constance, blows sexual experience and romantic love out of proportion. The Clerk's tale admits the place of sex in marriage, without coyness; nor does the Clerk suggest that Griselda's saintliness keeps her from enjoying sex. Rather, she is presented as a fertile mother and a loving wife:

> Nat longe tyme after that this Grisild
> Was wedded, she a doghter hath ybore.
> Al had hire levere have born a knave child...
> ....
> ...she nys nat bareyne.   (442-48)

After the daughter is taken away,

> As glad, as humble, as bisy in servyse,
> And eek in love, as she was wont to be,
> Was she to hym in every maner wyse.   (603-05)

The pattern repeats after Griselda's son is removed: "The moore trewe, if that it were possible, / She was to hym in love, and moore penyble" (713-14). Griselda speaks frankly about sex as a consecrated part of her marriage with Walter:

> For sith I yaf to yow my maydenhede,
> And am youre trewe wyf, it is no drede,
> God shilde swich a lordes wyf to take
> Another man to housbonde or to make!   (837-40)

She asks for a smock, when Walter turns her out, "in gerdon of my maydenhede, / Which that I broghte, and noght agayn I bere" (883-84), in order to "wrye the wombe of here / That was youre wyf" (887-88)—it seems improper, in her eyes, "That thilke wombe in which youre children leye" (877) should be seen bare before the people. These passages in the Clerk's tale all respond to the coy refusal to be frank about sex in the Man of Law's tale (II.708-14). But in the Clerk's tale sex in marriage assumes a place in a larger context, not becoming, as in the Wife's tale, the most important part of the marriage.

I think it is most instructive, then, to approach the Clerk's tale looking back through the Wife's tale, to the tale of Constance. There are many obvious parallels between the two quasi-saints' lives. Both tales have the reiterative folk-tale structure, and both heroines are tested for constancy.[30] But Constance's suffering is arbitrary, from the temporal perspective—

it is inflicted upon her by an inscrutable Providence. Griselda's suffering is, on the other hand, *voluntary*. It is the result of a vow freely taken, and everything she does exhibits her determination to live up to that vow. She says to Walter, when he "proposes,"

> ... as ye wole youreself, right so wol I.
> And heere I swere that nevere willyngly,
> In werk ne thoght, I nyl yow disobeye,
> For to be deed, though me were looth to deye.   (361-64)

One critic argues that Griselda becomes "almost the apotheosis of the philosophical concept of the *patiens*, the thing-being-acted-upon."[31] Though Griselda at times seems to fit this description, I think we must always remember that what she does is a result of an *action* upon her part, a freely taken oath. This initial oath changes all of her subsequent suffering into action, as well. She is doing something, living up to her vow and therefore imposing upon her world the order she has freely willed it to have.

Nor is Griselda ever passive or detached, like Constance. Besides gladly producing heirs, she is an active ruler, an able administrator and a good judge: "The commune profit koude she redresse. / Ther nas discord, rancour, ne hevynesse" (431-32); "So wise and rype wordes hadde she, / And juggementz of so greet equitee" (438-39). Griselda's hard work as her father's housekeeper is later mirrored in her cheerful "bisynesse" when she adorns the chamber of Walter's "bride" (974 ff.). This work, as with her instruction of Walter in how to treat high-born women (1037-43), is not suffering, but doing. As she herself tells Walter, "I wol no thyng, ne nyl no thyng, certayn, / But as yow list" (646-47). The key to Griselda's character, perhaps, is less her patience than her *bountee*, her generosity or magnanimity of soul, a theme the Clerk's tale sounds again and again: "Hir bountee" (244); "thewes goode, yset in heigh bountee" (409); "the bountee of hire name" (415); "of hire heighe bountee the fame" (418).

Bountee is the willingness to grant others freedom to be what they are. It is not exactly self-abnegation, as in Whittock's reading.[32] But Whittock is surely correct in observing that the intrusive passages critical of Walter's behavior attack *maistrie* itself, "the domination and exploitation of any human being by another" (p. 149). The theme of freedom appears everywhere in the tale. Besides the passages about Griselda's freedom or lack of it, there is Walter's irresponsible freedom from marriage at the beginning (80 ff.); there are his discussion of marriage as a loss of liberty (145 ff.) and his attempt to preserve his freedom by choosing as he pleases (150 ff.); there are Walter's assertions that his political position constrains him to do things he would prefer not to do (490, 624 ff., 796 ff.); there is the sergeant's speech about the necessity of obeying lords (526-32); and so on. The freedom that is so important to Walter is precisely what he tries to take away from Griselda. But he does not succeed, for by the agency of her vow Griselda has assured that her own freedom lies in obedience to Walter. In short, the experience recounted in the tale is valuable to Griselda, not just because it ends happily, but because it gives scope to her virtue of *bountee*.

Walter is the one who initiates the experience, however; he wants "Fully to han experience and loore / If that she were as stidefast as bifoore" (788-89). The experience is also valuable and significant to Walter, because he at last understands the depth of his wife's *bountee* and the meaning of freedom within the marriage relationship:

> "Grisilde," quod he, "by God, that for us deyde,
> Thou art my wyf, ne noon oother I have,
> Ne nevere hadde, as God my soule save!"   (1062-64)

Walter here seems also to be renouncing the possibility that he would wish *not* to be married to Griselda, a significant progression from the carefree attitude of the hawker and hunter in the beginning of the story.

The Clerk's tale, then, is a proper answer to the Man of Law's tale, correcting the excesses of the Wife's attempt. The Clerk's tale shows that earthly experience is valuable and significant, and it does so by taking the disputation to the Man of Law's own camp with another story about a virtuous, suffering woman.

But of course, the Clerk's tale has always been one of the least satisfying—to modern critics, anyway. On the human level, the story is incredible or outrageous, as the Clerk himself admits (1142 ff.). Like the Clerk, critics excuse these difficulties by pointing away from the fable and toward the moral of the tale.[33] But in his pitying comments and his intrusive denunciations of Walter, the Clerk himself also invites and endorses a response to the story on the human level. Some modern critics read the apparent failures of the tale dramatically—the Clerk is revealed as sentimentalist or unsophisticated artist.[34] Whether one accepts the dramatic reading or not, the points of such critics are well taken. On the human level, *bountee* such as Griselda's is never found; and if it were found, it would never work. The end of the Clerk's tale, and the Envoy, say as much. But in a sense, it is too late, because our experience of the tale has already shown us as much. Unless we escape upwards into the allegorical, Walter and Griselda are too much to swallow. Life is not really the way the tale portrays it, because human beings are not God. Husbands do not "assay" their wives—they exploit them, if anything.

And wives, if they are able, exploit their husbands. That is what the Merchant's tale shows us.

The Merchant's Tale

A great deal of critical energy has been spent in pointing out the many ways in which the Merchant's tale answers the Clerk's.[35] Despite broad agreement on some things, however, the Merchant's tale remains one of the more controversial. The question central in the controversy is whether the tale is "bitter," but that question gets confused with the question of whether to read dramatically or thematically. Critics have tried to show that the tale is not bitter, because the bitter Merchant is not the speaker;[36] or that it is bitter, because the bitter Merchant is the speaker;[37] or that it is not bitter, because, although the Merchant is the speaker, he is not bitter.[38] But of course, the tale could be "bitter" in one sense whether the Merchant is the speaker or not, and whether he is bitter or not. Insofar as we are dealing with a controversy about dramatic or thematic reading, the controversy is undecidable. The evidence adduced on either side already presupposes a generic commitment.

In my own reading, the Merchant's tale embodies a world-view that can be taken seriously. But, like every previous world-view in *The Canterbury Tales*, the world-view of the Merchant's tale is provisional. I am dissatisfied with the world-view and, perhaps, ultimately laugh at it—not with the scorn reserved for fools like January, but with relief at being able to get outside this dismal world-view. Whereas the Clerk's tale is about maintaining one's freedom and spiritual integrity by submitting to authority, the Merchant's tale is about losing one's freedom and spiritual integrity by exploiting another human being.

In this sense, the Merchant's tale directly answers the Clerk's—by portraying things as they "really are." Like Walter, January plays God; like Griselda, May is sorely tried. But there the resemblances end. January "made a gardyn, walled al with stoon" (2029), his Paradise; he sings to May with the "olde lewed wordes" (2149) of the Song of Solomon. January is "lewed," of course, to place himself in the role of *sponsus* in the Song, who in the various exegetical traditions is always God the Father or Christ.[39] January's projected forming of May, who is supposed to be like "warm wex" (1430) because she is young, is parodied in May's imprinting of the key to the garden in "warm wex" (2117), something she does ultimately because she is young. January wants to place himself in the position of the creator, and yet he wants the creature's enjoyment of the creation.[40] The wonderful reiteration of

65

corage (e.g., 1254, 1725, 1759, 1808) whereby it comes to mean "courage," "heart," and "sexual potency" all at once, suggests that sex for January is a kind of exploitation. His lip-smacking over "Oold fissh and yong flessh" (1418) prepares for his lascivious and revolting mock-sorrow over taking May's virginity. Imagery of knives and warfare suggests that for January the thought of sexual conquest is as titillating as the thought of sensual pleasure:

> But in his herte he gan hire to manace
> That he that nyght in armes wolde hire streyne
> Harder than evere Parys did Eleyne.
> But nathelees yet hadde he greet pitee
> That thilke nyght offenden hire moste he,
> And thoughte, "Allas! O tendre creature,
> Now wolde God ye myghte wel endure
> Al my corage, it is so sharp and keene!" (1752-59)

These are the tears of the Walrus as he gobbles the oysters. Later, in bed,

> He rubbeth hire aboute hir tendre face,
> And seyde thus, "Allas! I moot trespace
> To yow, my spouse, and yow greetly offende...
> ....
> A man may do no synne with his wyf,
> Ne hurte hymselven with his owene knyf." (1827-40)

The palpable folly of this last couplet, in its context, is so disgusting that we can work up a case of sympathy for May. And yet, she obviously exploits January as much as he exploits her. She is strongly contrasted with Griselda. When January orders her to "strepen hire al naked," she "obeyeth, be hire lief or looth" (1958-61), but all the time she is thinking about Damian. She decides in Damian's favor:

> "Certeyn," thoghte she, "whom that this thyng displese,
> I rekke noght, for heere I hym assure
> To love him best of any creature,
> Though he namoore hadde than his sherte." (1982-85)

May is not so unconcerned with January's possessions. He buys her, as the narrator makes clear in speaking of "every scrit and bond / By which that she was feffed in his lond" (1697-98), and as January recognizes when he lists—clearly in climactic order—the things that May will gain by being true to him:

Beth to me trewe, and I wol telle you why.
Thre thynges, certes, shal ye wynne therby:
First, love of Crist, and to youreself honour,
And al my heritage, toun and tour.   (2169-72)

May's bold-faced lies (2188-206, and at the end of the story) are
matched only by Damian's fawning hypocrisy:

And eek to Januarie he gooth as lowe
As evere did a dogge for the bowe.
He is so plesant unto every man
(For craft is al, whoso that do it kan).   (2013-16)

This last line, which might serve as a moral for this tale about a world of
mutual exploitation, makes a dirty word out of *craft*, as the earlier puns
have made a dirty word out of *corage*. In the world-view of the tale,
human skill is no more admirable than the devious and corrupted
human heart.

The Merchant's tale, then, answers the Clerk's by showing that
human relationships are mutually exploitative. But it also answers the
Clerk's tale in somewhat the same way that the Friar's tale answers the
Wife's, and on the same issue—the value and significance of human
experience. Experience is valuable to Griselda and significant to Walter;
but the characters in the Merchant's tale neither achieve scope for good
through experience, nor learn anything. Pluto, interestingly enough,
states clearly what the value of experience ought to be for January:

"My wyf," quod he, "ther may no wight seye nay;
Th' experience so preveth every day
The tresons whiche that wommen doon to man."   (2237-39)

And, interestingly enough, Pluto is overborne by Proserpina, just as
January is overborne by May,[41] even though the experience of the tale
does indicate that both Pluto and January are right about (some)
women's faithlessness. Meanwhile, Proserpina's argument concludes
with a statement that might well be aimed at the Clerk's idealization of
Griselda's virtue, *bountee*: "in sovereyn bontee / Nis noon but God, but
neither he ne she" (2289-90). Critics have always pointed out how
January's willful intellectual blindness is mirrored in his physical
blindness. Charles A. Owen, Jr., goes further and argues, I think
defensibly, that the story is "essentially the growth of an idea to
complete fulfillment."[42] The idea is January's notion of marriage as an
earthly paradise, and it is completely foolish. At the end, January is a
complete fool. And he is that because he is unwilling to pay attention to
experience—literally, unwilling to believe his own eyes.

Ironically, January thinks he is totally committed to the value of experience. He espouses a false and shallow Epicureanism (much as May and Damian seem to do): he "lyved in greet prosperitee" (1247); he "folwed ay his bodily delyt / On wommen, ther as was his appetyt" (1249-50). The principle is even elevated to the level of a philosophy for him:

> Somme clerkes holden that felicitee
> Stant in delit, and therfore certeyn he,
> This noble Januarie, with al his myght,
> In honest wyse, as longeth to a knyght,
> Shoop hym to lyve ful deliciously.   (2021-25)

But in spite of this dedication to pleasurable earthly experience, many of January's pleasures in the story seem to be more refined and mental. The tale never really dwells on the physical pleasure January gets from May. January *says* that he feels his "lymes stark and suffisaunt" (1458) and that his "corage" is "sharp and keene," but when he gets to bed the description is all of pawing and talk. There is little explicit commentary on other action: "Thus laboureth he til that the day gan dawe" (1842)— the reader is not told whether the labor succeeds or fails. When Damian goes to work, however, it is far otherwise: "And sodeynly anon this Damyan / Gan pullen up the smok, and in he throng" (2352-53). From the beginning of the story, January is stronger in imagination ("fantasye") than in deeds or in rational thought:

> Heigh fantasye and curious bisynesse
> Fro day to day gan in the soule impresse
> Of Januarie aboute his mariage.   (1577-79)

(See also, for example, lines 1580-88, 1600 ff., and 1610.) When he is sitting at the marriage feast with May, he imagines what he is going to do: "This Januarie is ravysshed in a traunce" (1750). His "outrageous" jealousy (2087), of course, for all that he knows, is just another fantasy. And the supreme achievement of his imagination is to imagine that May's preposterous excuse is true. Thus January, committed as he is to experience, is a fool because he does not learn anything from it. Experience is valuable and significant, but man's imagination or fantasy prevents him from seeing what the world is really like.[43]

Justinus is the obvious exception in the tale. He affirms the value of judging by experience, as opposed to judging by what people say:

> And yet, God woot, my neighebores aboute,
> And namely of wommen many a route,

> Seyn that I have the mooste stedefast wyf,
> And eek the mekeste oon that bereth lyf;
> But I woot best where wryngeth me my sho.
> Ye mowe, for me, right as you liketh do.   (1549-54)

Ironically, however, Justinus' own negative advice renders itself powerless when it is confronted with determined folly. Justinus suggests that one should judge from one's own experience—therefore, all advice, Justinus' included, is of secondary importance. Placebo suggests the same thing—the lords will do what they wish, anyway, so why cross them? Justinus' second piece of advice—in which he says to January, essentially, "You'll see for yourself," is motivated by his hatred of January's folly (1655). Justinus' point is that January should consider the realities for himself. But in the world of the tale, folly cannot be corrected by good advice, because the only good advice one man can give another is the advice not to be foolish—to judge wisely from one's own experience. Folly thus has a built-in protection from listening to good advice, as Placebo's principles implicitly recognize.

Tatlock said long ago that one meaning of the Merchant's tale is "the inexorable chastisement for stubborn shutting the eyes to facts"; Tatlock called this moral a "sound if one-sided philosophy."[44] Whittock seconds the point: the tale, "as far as it goes, is a valid comment on life," but its teller is limited because his interests are "materialistic and self-centered."[45] Alfred David and, more recently, Emerson Brown argue that the point of view of the tale is created by Chaucer to represent a part of himself that he wishes specifically to reject. For David, the tale is a "chilling illustration of what happens to satire when it is divorced from humanity and employed as the weapon of misanthropy";[46] Brown suggests that the tale is a "palinode, or recantation, in this case a summoning to judgment of a lifetime of antifeminist raillery," where Chaucer confesses an "awareness of the ugly springs from which misogynistic wit flows."[47] Without necessarily accepting a dramatic reading or the biographical hypothesis, I think we can see in the statements of these critics something of what is unsatisfactory in the world-view the Merchant's tale shows us. There is, once again, too little room for the good things about human beings to emerge and be given their due. Fragment V gives the other side of the picture, including the Squire's tale and the Franklin's tale, both of which take human life as a beautiful and elevating spectacle.

The Squire's Tale

I shall not pause long over the Squire's tale, though in some respects it represents some of the most interesting critical problems in *The Canterbury Tales*. Most of the controversy concerns whether the tale is complete as it stands—whether, that is, Chaucer intended for the Franklin to interrupt the Squire. Some argue that the tale would have been finished, if Chaucer had lived.[48] Others argue that the interruption is deliberate, either giving the young Squire welcome release from a test of his tale-telling ability;[49] or gently rebuking the Squire's values;[50] or implicitly criticizing the genre of the romance, which in the Squire's hands has gotten out of control.[51] To attempt to decide whether the Franklin interrupts the Squire, however, already presupposes a dramatic reading. Therefore, I shall pass by the question, except to say that if I were the Franklin, I would certainly have interrupted the Squire—and precisely at the point where the tale ends, when almost nothing important has happened after six hundred lines, and when the catalog in lines 661-69 of narratives in store seems to promise a performance of nearly infinite length.[52]

The Squire's tale as it stands has interesting verbal and thematic resonances with other tales.[53] I am most interested, however, in the relationship of the Squire's tale with the immediately preceding tale. There are a number of curious verbal echoes of the Merchant's tale. For example, the "motto" of the Merchant's tale in line 2016 ("For craft is al . . .") is echoed in the lines about the inability of courtiers to move the magic horse:

> Ther may no man out of the place it dryve
> For noon engyn of wyndas or polyve;
> And cause why? for they kan nat the craft.   (183-85)

The Squire's sentiment superficially agrees with the Merchant's, but the Squire also implies that there are subtleties in "craft" that some will always remain incapable of understanding. As the Squire says in lines 221-24,

> . . . lewed peple demeth comunly
> Of thynges that been maad moore subtilly
> Than they kan in hir lewednesse comprehende;
> They demen gladly to the badder ende.

Though the immediate context is the ignorant comments about the magic horse, I read the lines as directed against the presumption of the Merchant's tale, which satirizes the intricate code of courtly love and through ignorance of real love judges "gladly to the badder ende."

Somewhat similarly, January's ravishment at May and the allusion to Paris and Helen (1750-54) are echoed in the lines describing the false tercelet's swearing of love to the falcon: "So ravysshed, as it semed, for the joye, / That nevere Jason ne Parys of Troye" (547-48). The point in the Squire's tale, however, is precisely that the tercelet is a hypocrite and a dissembler. He is not at all "lyk a gentil lovere" (546), as he appears to be—and the same comment would apply, in a different sense, to January. The tercelet is more like Damian. Just as Damian "kembeth hym, he preyneth hym and pyketh" (2011), so the tercelet "peynted . . . and kembde at point-devys" (560), and both of the two are hypocrites. Damian is the serpent in the tree in January's false Paradise; he is also the "servant traytour, false hoomly hewe, / Lyk to the naddre in bosom sly untrewe" (1785-86). Similarly, the hypocritical tercelet "Right as a serpent hit hym under floures / Til he may seen his tyme for to byte" (512-13). And finally, as has often been noted, that famous line about pity and the gentle heart links the Squire's tale not only to the Knight's tale (line 1761), but also to the ironic comment on May's "gentilesse" in lines 1986 and following of the Merchant's tale. The falcon tells Canacee,

> That pitee renneth soone in gentil herte,
> Feelynge his similitude in peynes smerte,
> Is preved alday, as men may it see,
> As wel by werk as by auctoritee;
> For gentil herte kitheth gentillesse. (479-83)

The lines of course implicitly excoriate May's falseness, but they also implicitly rebuke the irony of the Merchant's tale. For the Squire's tale, it is true that pity is an attribute of a truly gentle heart, and in a truly gentle heart pity is not confused with lust. So while the Squire's tale affirms the Merchant's disapproval of falseness in men and women, it rejects the Merchant's irony and cynicism.

It makes sense, then, to see the Squire's tale as an answer to the Merchant's tale, as several critics have done.[54] I should prefer, however, to read the tale as a comment on the central theme of fragments III-V— the value and significance of human experience. And as usual, the world-view exhibited in the Squire's tale is satisfying in some ways and unsatisfactory in others.

In the Squire's tale we are shown human experience as a spectacle to be contemplated. That stance toward the world is typical of the romance-genre. We are shown, moreover, two different ways of contemplating experience, one invalid and the other valid. As I have already suggested, the reactions of the bystanders to the magical gifts represent a foolish, inane sort of contemplation. As the Squire says, "They demen gladly to the badder ende," because in their "lewednesse" they cannot understand what they are seeing. The verb that the Squire uses elsewhere to describe their talk is to "jangle" (lines 257, 261, for example), suggesting the valuelessness, the inanity, of their contemplation of experience. This episode answers the Merchant's worm's-eye view that, failing to understand what it sees, sees everything for the worst. But another kind of contemplation is exhibited in the tale. That is Canacee's contemplation of the falcon's experience. Canacee does not "jangle" or judge "to the badder ende." Instead, she has compassion (462-63) because, as the falcon says, "gentil herte kitheth gentillesse." Valid contemplation of human (or avian) experience requires an investment of the self, an emotional involvement. The kind of experience Canacee is contemplating is an extremely attenuated sort of thing—the courtly-love affair of a bird. It takes a truly "gentil" heart to enter into valid contemplation of what most people would reject as foolishness (see the *Parliament of Fowles*, 596-602). But this is precisely the point. The value of human experience is as a spectacle to be contemplated, and so experience can have value only to the extent that one is capable (through gentility or refinement of perception) of valid contemplation. This is what the incomplete tale shows us.

Just as the frequent use of *occupatio* in the Knight's tale shows the narrator's concern for imposing order on a tale that is about order, so the Squire's more frequent use of the same device reinforces the theme of the value of human experience. One difference between the Knight's use of *occupatio* and the Squire's is that the Squire ineptly calls attention to himself rather than to the grandeur of his story.[55] But I should add the observation that the Squire's *occupatio* differs from the Knight's in that we get the notion that the Knight *could* competently tell about the things he passes over, if he would; whereas the Squire is continually denying his ability to tell about things (e.g., lines 72, 105-06, 279-90, 342-43, 424). Nor, judging from the things he does tell about, do we have much warrant to suppose that the Squire is underestimating his abilities. But the point is that the Squire is continually telling us, in essence, "You had to be there"—the things he describes are things that have to be properly contemplated in person to be understood. Thus, the device of *occupatio* on one level serves a similar function in this tale and in the Knight's tale. The device in the Knight's tale exhibits a narrator's ordering of a tale about order; in the Squire's tale the device shows a narrator experiencing a tale about experience.

But of course, as critics have often said, there is ultimately something silly about the experience in the Squire's tale. Not only the posturings of courtly love[56] are silly. Nor is it just the Squire's rhetorical self-indulgence[57] or his surrendering to the illusions of fiction[58] or his youthful innocence or narcissism.[59] All of these notions are certainly there. But I would emphasize another point. Critics have noticed that the wonderful gifts are apparently the key to the tale, but that the Squire fails to discuss the significance of the gifts.[60] The inconclusive discussion of the gifts serves only to call attention to the fact that they never get explained; nor is there any indication that the Squire is going to explain them. Similarly, the story of the falcon seems to go nowhere.[61] The point is that experience in the world-view of the Squire's tale does not lack significance in any absolute sense, but it *seems* to lack significance, to "go nowhere," because in the contemplative stance the tale recommends, everything is on the same level with everything else. Life is a pageant that unrolls before one's eyes, but the events in the pageant might be unconnected with each other, might not move to narrative crisis. What is before one's eyes at any moment is all-absorbing. Such a world is all phenomenon and no law. No principle gives coherence to events or makes distinctions of relative importance. A bird crossed in love is placed on the same level as magic gifts that allow men to overcome the limitations of time and space, to look into other minds, and to wield irresistible power. And all of this is apparently going to be put on the same level with war, death, and human love. And that is what is ultimately unsatisfying about the world-view of the Squire's tale. Human experience still has value as spectacle—positive, emotionally elevating value, unlike the experience of the Merchant's tale—and there are right ways and wrong ways to contemplate the spectacle. But there is no way to make distinctions among the matters available for contemplation. The Franklin's tale, which follows, is a tale about, among other things, making distinctions.

The Franklin's Tale

Critics have often quarreled over whether the Franklin's tale is "Chaucer's solution" to the "marriage-debate." The quarrel obscures a deeper issue. To say that the tale represents Chaucer's solution, even in a dramatic reading, we have to have decided already that the world-view of the tale is endorsed by Chaucer; on the other hand, to say that the tale cannot be Chaucer's solution is to argue that the world-view of the tale is somehow invalid for Chaucer. The fundamental issue, then, is the extent to which the Franklin's tale exhibits a valid world-view. We are in a situation similar to that of the Knight's tale. With the Knight's tale, dramatic readings tend to explain how the Knight's vision of order is valid, because in a dramatic reading the function of the tale is to portray a character whom we know from the frame-story to be an ideal. Thematic readings, on the other hand, tend to concentrate on the limitations of the Knight's vision, because thematic readings are concerned to show that any world-view is just one of a number of contenders. Since the Franklin is not clearly an ideal character, we have a similar equation, but with the signs reversed. The Franklin, though basically admirable, does have contradictions in his character. He is genial but pretentious, deferential but upwardly mobile, Christian but Epicurean. Dramatic readings of his tale, then, tend to focus on the deficiencies in his world-view that account for some of these contradictions in his character.[62] Thematic readings concentrate on showing how his world-view has its own validity—though we might see limitations in that world-view by contrasting it with others.[63] To the extent that opposed generic orientations determine opposed readings, the controversy is undecidable. We have, not genuine controversy about the state of affairs, but a critical dialectic that comes from adopting different interpretive systems.[64]

According to my usual principle, I shall set aside the question of the ultimate validity of the world-view (an undecidable question) and the related question of the marriage debate.[65] Instead, I shall look at the world-view in the context of the others presented in the other tales. I shall try to see how the world-view takes its place as a part of the reader's experience of the whole work—that is, see what use the tale is put to by the reader as he attempts to see *The Canterbury Tales* whole.

Certainly the Franklin's tale answers the Wife's (and the other tales in the traditional Marriage Group) on the subject of *maistrie*. But as several critics have pointed out,[66] the tale involves a much larger context than that of the putative marriage-debate. Just as the Clerk looks back through the Wife's answer to the Man of Law to construct a better answer, so the Franklin looks back through the Squire's answer to the Merchant. The Franklin's idealism answers the Merchant's cynicism, certainly. Instead of mutual exploitation in the love-triangle, we have mutual forbearance; instead of hypocrisy and breaking of vows, we have *trouthe* upheld and followed as the highest human ideal. This elevation of *trouthe* in Arveragus' statement that "Trouthe is the hyeste thyng that man may kepe" (1479) represents a setting of priorities that makes the Franklin's tale also an answer to the Squire's tale. *Trouthe* was upheld in the Squire's tale as a value, certainly—it would have been better for the tercelet to be true than false—but the value of the falcon's experience as matter for Canacee's contemplation is not dependent one way or the other on *trouthe*. Presumably, a courtly-love story about birds in which

74

both were true would have been equally interesting. The potential value of experience in the Franklin's tale is different, however, depending upon whether *trouthe* is upheld or betrayed. Experience is not merely the matter of contemplation. It is the opportunity to act in the world, to make a human world over as we would have it to be. As Harry Berger, Jr., suggests,[67] even the contemplation of experience must find its justification in the use to which that contemplation is put. The Franklin's *demande* at the end has precisely the effect of forcing us to make distinctions, even subtle ones—whether or not we can decide finally who is most "free," we must at least consider the possibilities and attempt to impose significant hierarchy on the experience we have contemplated. Emotional involvement like Canacee's with our experience is not enough. So the Franklin seems to be suggesting that we need a more powerful answer to the Merchant than the Squire provides. The Franklin thus, adopting the Clerk's tactic, tells a "similar" story from the perspective of a different world-view—and shows how the world is different from what the Merchant portrays.[68]

A curious echo of the Summoner's tale reinforces the point. When Arveragus hears Dorigen's story of her folly, his answer might seem strange: "Is ther oght elles, Dorigen, but this?" (1469). The line echoes the lady in the Summoner's tale, who responds to Friar John's angry recital, "Is ther oght elles? telle me feithfully" (2203). The contrast is clear. The sense of the lady's question is to dismiss Friar John's complaint as something trivial and in any case something sparked by an irrational action for which there is no accounting and no remedy. The best thing to do, she says, is to ignore it. Arveragus is not saying that at all, though his form of speech calls attention to itself precisely because of the momentary shock we get when we think he might be dismissing Dorigen's experience as trivial. In fact, this is a serious matter to him, as his weeping in line 1480 indicates. We have a strong contrast between the dismissing of a trivial action, and the exercise of forbearance in dealing with an extremely important action. Tolerance is necessary in human relations, because "Ire, siknesse, or constellacioun, / Wyn, wo, or chaungynge of complexioun"—that is, both things within our control and things beyond it—"Causeth ful ofte to doon amys or speken" (781-83). Arveragus seems to be asking Dorigen about the state of her soul. He wants to know if she has told all of her feelings. If she has, then the important matter is settled—she is spiritually true to Arveragus in spite of her promise. Unlike January and May, Arveragus and Dorigen care for each other's feelings; unlike the characters in the Squire's tale, they take experience as something more than a beautiful surface.

Everyone in the tale learns something from the experience. Arveragus learns about the flightiness of his wife and, perhaps, about how generous a squire can be. Dorigen learns something about the folly of questioning the natural order, and a great deal about her husband, Aurelius, and herself. Aurelius learns how noble Arveragus can be, and in turn learns the heights he himself can rise to. And the clerk learns how bright the world can be when people are as noble as Arveragus and Aurelius. There are, the clerk discovers, some things more important than a thousand pounds.

The enemy in the tale is illusion. The Franklin himself, in a speech that might seem gently to rebuke the Wife's satirical sally against the friars, says, "hooly chirches feith in oure bileve / Ne suffreth noon illusioun us to greve" (1133-34). Dorigen's fear for Arveragus is described as a "derke fantasye" (844). There is Dorigen's illusion that the "grisly feendly rokkes blake" are not congruent with the creation of which they are a part:

> In ydel, as men seyn, ye no thyng make.
> But, Lord, thise grisly feendly rokkes blake,
> That semen rather a foul confusioun
> Of werk than any fair creacion
> Of swich a parfit wys God and a stable,
> Why han ye wroght this werk unresonable?   (867-72)

This sort of idle speculation leads Dorigen into the rash promise. Then there are the illusions the clerk produces for Aurelius and his brother, all of which show how "one figure preys upon another" and which conclude with an illusion of Aurelius himself, dancing with Dorigen.[69] The illusion of the disappearance of the rocks astonishes and frightens Dorigen. Ironically, she who prayed for the incongruous rocks to be gone now objects to their disappearance because "It is agayns the proces of nature" (1345)—she affirms the natural order that she earlier questioned.[70]

The significance of experience in the tale is to dispel illusion. Dorigen's "complaint," so-called, has been the occasion for a minor critical controversy, some critics arguing that her multiple exempla should serve primarily to amuse us, and some arguing that all the examples are well chosen and apposite to her situation.[71] I think the cue comes in line 1457: "Thus pleyned Dorigen a day or tweye," where the narrator, tongue in cheek, seems to suggest that the length of the complaint makes little difference, since the same result will occur in any case. Dorigen is escaping from her situation and talking herself out of suicide. We should place the "complaint" in the context of all the other "sermons" that do not accomplish their ostensible goals in this group of tales—the hag's

76

sermon to the knight, the devil-yeoman's description of hell, Friar John's sermon on wrath, Walter's discourses to Griselda on the duties of a prince (which miss the mark because Griselda has promised to obey Walter anyway), Justinus' advice to January, and the inconclusive speculations of the courtiers about the magical gifts in the Squire's tale. In all of these cases, either the intent of the speaker(s) is hidden or in fact contrary to the purpose of the speech, or the person(s) addressed fail to profit from the speech, or both. In Dorigen's case, she is both speaker and audience, and both of the generalizations hold. The experience of confronting Aurelius is worth more to Dorigen (and the others) than all the authorities she can muster in two days of complaining. The women in the exempla are dead, and their virture is fixed and unchangeable. Dorigen's virtue, however, still has scope. It is at risk, to be sure, but the value of human experience is to allow Dorigen and the others in the tale to become as good as they can be.

And that leaves us with the grisly rocks. The Franklin's tale, as the last tale in its group, should clearly prepare the way for the next group. It does so by bringing into clear focus for the first time a problem that has been implicit in every tale in the group. All of the finished tales in this group may end in laughter for the reader: indulgent laughter at the young knight in the Wife's tale, grim laughter at the summoner who is carried off to hell, scornful laughter at Friar John or January, and laughter of delight that accompanies the ending of the Clerk's tale or the Franklin's tale. We perhaps even chuckle when the Franklin interrupts the Squire, if we believe that he does. And all of the tales except the Summoner's fabliau have about them the atmosphere of the fairy tale or the folk tale. But, as critics have said again and again in discussing the tales of this group, life is not a fairy tale. Life is not like a fairy tale, because we cannot live an hour reflectively without being confronted with the problem of evil. This, I think, is the problem that the Franklin's tale brings into sharp focus and that the next fragment (the Physician's tale and the Pardoner's tale) picks up to harp on.

The rocks in the Franklin's tale represent the problem of evil, as the speech of Dorigen's quoted earlier makes clear. Some see the Franklin's tale as a theodicy,[72] but others are not so sanguine. Ruggiers, for example, says that Dorigen voices "the frightening possibility of collision between the freedoms of created things";[73] and Bryant Bachman finds in the tale a "dual perspective"—first, the Boethian view that apparent evil is illusory, and second, the experiential view in which evil is stubbornly present.[74] For Bachman, the disappearance of the rocks represents the Boethian solution to the problem of evil—we alter our perception, and evil disappears. But in the tale, the rocks *are* still there.

Dorigen's reaction to their disappearance suggests "the difficulty of accepting the Boethian resolution to the problem of evil" (p. 64).

And indeed, it is a difficulty. At the root of the criticism that finds the Franklin's world-view limited is precisely this sense that everything is somehow too easy, that the problem of evil is too easily dealt with here, and, in retrospect, in the other tales of the group. What about the maiden who is raped in the Wife's tale? What about the summoner's victims and Thomas' sickness? What about Griselda's years of thinking her children are dead? What about January's blindness? What about the falcon's suffering, which for Canacee is merely an occasion for pity? And what would have happened if Aurelius had *not* repented? As with the rocks, all of these matters are more or less swept aside by rhetorical magic—now you see them, now you don't. In their concentration on the value of earthly experience, the tales have tried to ignore an important part of that experience, which now obtrudes itself upon our attention in the form of the grisly rocks. What we have is something very much like Marianne Moore's "imaginary gardens with real toads in them"—we have a fairy tale with real rocks. As much as we would like to rest in the world-view of the Franklin's tale, there is no way we can do so for long, for there is no vantage-point in the tale from which the grisly rocks are not part of the prospect. Alfred David puts the point elegantly: "The weakness of the Franklin's 'freedom,' whether we look at it as a Christian or a courtly virtue, is that no one has to pay. The Franklin's tale is, like the art of the clerk of Orleans, superficial. The obstacles disappear from sight, but they remain ever-present below the surface."[75]

CHAPTER SIX

Fragment VI:
The Problem of Evil

When we move from fragment V to fragment VI, we move from a fairy-tale world into a stifling atmosphere of irremediable evil. Critics have suggested that the theme of fragment VI is death;[1] or that the Host's words in the Physician-Pardoner link about the "yiftes of Fortune and of Nature" (295) indicate the unifying theme—both tales are about the detriment or the abuse of the gifts of Fortune, Nature, and grace.[2] Certainly these themes are prominent in the fragment, but I think they are just particular manifestations of the major concern of both tales— namely the problem of evil. The Physician's tale and the Pardoner's tale are both reactions against the happy endings, the superficiality, of the preceding tales. They both show us a world where evil, incomprehensible and incurable, is on the loose. It is not swept out of sight like the black rocks, nor is it an illusion to be dispelled. It is a brute, irresistible fact of creation that sweeps the human beings in the tales before it. Both Physician's and Pardoner's tales are in a sense cruel, because they remind the pilgrims (and the reader) of things we would rather forget. The tales are very short on *solaas*, but their tellers are careful to buttress their performances with unexceptionable *sentence*, from behind which they can mock at the discomfiture of the audience.

It is important that both tales make certain kinds of truth-claims. The Physician claims historical truth:

> ... this is no fable,
> But knowen for historial thyng notable;
> The sentence of it sooth is, out of doute.... (155-57)

The Pardoner's tale, he claims, is part of the sermon he has by rote. That is, he is reproducing for the pilgrims words that have actually been spoken in various churches in his territory. The Physician's claim is that life was once unalterably as he portrays it; the Pardoner's claim is that life is and will continue to be as he portrays it, since his tale is not fictive with respect to the frame—it is a recital of recent events, self-quotation. The world of the Pardoner's tale is not the fictive world of story, he maintains, which winks into existence when a story is being told and

79

winks out when the story ends. It is not even the world of historical fact that is at least distanced by time. It is the world of the fourteenth-century pilgrims to whom he speaks, the world of here and now. Both these tales suggest that the world of story is one thing, whereas the real world is another. And the difference is that in the real world, evil often triumphs.

The Physician's Tale

The Physician's tale answers the Franklin's in that both are about women whose chastity is assailed. But Dorigen's case ends happily, Virginia's unhappily. Several critics have pointed out that Dorigen's complaint talks about women like Virginia;[3] the connection between the tales has been used to argue for the Ellesmere order[4] and to argue that one point of the tale is to put "into its proper light the shallowness of Dorigen's character."[5] Dorigen complains for a day or two, and then chooses not to kill herself; Virginia chooses death in short order.

But there are other resonances between the two tales. In the Franklin's tale the problem of evil assumes the form of the grisly rocks, which Dorigen contemplates as examples of natural evil. When the rocks disappear, she cries, "It is agayns the proces of nature." We have a neat reversal of the theme in the Physician's insistence on Virginia's beauty as a paragon of Nature (lines 9-13). Virginia's beauty is an exact opposition to the ugliness of the grisly rocks. The rocks seem to show nature working against man, hostile to human life. Virginia seems to show nature as the fostering creatress who holds man up as her crowning achievement. And yet, Virginia's beauty causes Appius' crime: "So was he caught with beautee of this mayde" that "Anon the feend into his herte ran" (127, 130). The tale does more than to arouse our pity because of Virginia's beauty or to point out that the gifts of nature can be detrimental to their possessor. It calls into question the easy assumption of the Franklin's tale that the appearance of evil is just the result of faulty perception. In the Franklin's tale we could say that Dorigen's perception of the rocks was inaccurate, and that apparent evil is really part of the Providential dispensation. In the Physician's tale, however, we cannot present a similar argument. Our perception of Nature is accurate—Virginia is beautiful; and yet human evil results from the *accuracy* of that perception. Natural evil does not play a role in the Physician's tale, but the tale suggests that for that very reason human evil is all the more obtrusive and incomprehensible. The "feend," notice, does not cause Appius to lust for Virginia. The "feend" merely shows Appius a plan for satisfying his lust.

Similarly, the Physician's digression on chaperones and parents has resonances with preceding tales. Virginia is not only beautiful. She has

Griselda's quality of *bountee* (110, 112, 136). For Griselda, suffering becomes occasion for the exercise of her *bountee*. But for Virginia, her *bountee* is precisely that magnanimity of soul that makes her choose death over dishonor:

> . . . she
> Confermed was in swich soverayn bountee,
> That wel he wiste he myghte hire nevere wynne
> As for to make hire with hir body synne.   (135-38)

Her *bountee*, then, is not what gives her scope for the exercise of virtue, but precisely what cuts her off before her time.

The function of guardians and parents, according to the Physician, is to *restrict* children. For Virginia, that means restriction of opportunities for expressing her *bountee*. The Physician indicates that sometimes those who "han falle in freletee" make better chaperones, because they "knowen wel ynough the olde daunce" (78-79). Dorigen could have used such a chaperone, perhaps to keep her away from the temptations of the dances that Virginia avoids (62-66),[6] and certainly to keep Aurelius from speaking. Arveragus, who has responsibility for the "governaunce" of Dorigen, is too free with her, in terms of the world-view of the Physician's tale. He leaves her alone, and imagines no problems; he sends her to Aurelius, giving her the freedom to bear the responsibility of her own actions. The Physician's tale rebukes such an attitude on the part of governors: "Looke wel that ye unto no vice assente" (87). The wise chaperone or parent, again, acts from an accurate perception, perhaps even from the knowledge gained through bitter experience. The Physician advises,

> Beth war, that by ensample of youre lyvynge,
> Or by youre necligence in chastisynge,
> That they ne perisse.   (97-99)

Ironically, however, Virginia perishes precisely *because* of her father's punctiliousness as a guardian of her virtue. Only in the world of the fairy tale could negligence like Arveragus' turn out all right. In the Physician's tale, we are not allowed the comfort of attributing suffering to faulty perception. Virginius' perception of his role is accurate, and the suffering in the tale arises precisely from that accurate perception. Virginia is caught between Appius' accurate perception of her beauty, and her father's accurate perception of his responsibility.[7] The problem of evil is genuine, and not just a matter of faulty or partial perception.

The Physician's tale, then, shows something different from what it says. Its moral is trite—"Heere may men seen how synne hath his

81

merite" (277)—and ironical, for the tale rather demonstrates how virtue attracts undeserved suffering.[8] The moral has seemed to some critics not to be apposite to the story at all.[9] The critics who attempt to find the tale morally uplifting[10] find themselves in a distinct minority. Typical comments are as follows. Whittock: "the Physician's moralising is glib and callous";[11] Ramsey: "the simple little moral tale has become a nightmare of contradictions";[12] Howard: the tale is "a dramatic example of misguided moralism: he praises virtue in a tale that is morally revolting."[13] The tale has always been offensive to critics, and would seem more so, were we to accept the interpretation of Jerome H. Mandel, who argues that by the political philosophy of Chaucer's time, Virginius would have been justified in calling on his many friends and rebelling against the tyrant[14]—in other words, Virginia need not have died for morality to be satisfied.

The offensiveness of the tale is not so much the moral insensitivity of its teller (as it would be in a dramatic reading), but instead the unpalatability of what it shows us about the problem of evil. The innocent die at the hands of the moral, and there is "no remedye" (236) for Virginia. Springing from the suggestion of the grisly rocks in the Franklin's tale, the Physician's tale shows us a world we find intolerable, and all the more so because it seems to correspond in crucial ways to the real world, the world of history and of contemporary experience.

The Pardoner's Tale

Most critics concentrate not on the Pardoner's tale itself, but on the endlessly fascinating problem of the Pardoner's own psychology. By now we have run through most of the permutations of the various mixtures of sincerity and outright gall in attempts to explain his outrageous behavior. Every now and again, an article appears that summarizes the criticism.[15] By far the most satisfying reading to me is Howard's. Howard treats the Pardoner as a "grotesque" who "acts the role given to him, becomes an embodiment, a charade of evil. And in doing this he reflects back to us the evil we dread in ourselves."[16] In a kind of "self-parody," the Pardoner avenges himself on the "good citizen" whose victim he is "by making the good citizen . . . question all cultural values and suspect all moral discourse of being cant" (p. 374).

It is perhaps more difficult to separate tale from teller here than it is anywhere else in *The Canterbury Tales*. That is another way of saying that the Pardoner's tale, as a sermon recited by rote, makes a claim to a kind of non-fictionality that most of the other tales do not make. It makes a claim to be read as a dramatic speech; and as sermon, the tale is part of the "real life" of the pilgrimage. Unlike the Wife's tale, the Pardoner's is an integral part of his "confession."[17] In short, the non-fictionality of the Pardoner's sermon shows us that the world of his tale is *the* world. The rascal on the pilgrimage is as bad as the rascals in the exemplum. The Pardoner's performance turns the screw a little tighter than the Physician's tale did. No longer is irremediable evil confined to the world of the distant past. Even if the Host, the pilgrims, and the reader turn against the Pardoner, his presence reminds us of the evil of our world, thrust obscenely before our eyes.[18]

The world of the tale is above all a world of waste. The sins of the tavern are wasteful sins. Gluttony is exemplary. Through gluttony Adam wasted his opportunity to live in Paradise (505 ff.). Cooks "stampe, and streyne, and grynde, / And turnen substaunce into accident" (538-39) in order to please the "stynkyng cod, / Fulfilled of dong and of corrupcioun" (534-35). Their work is destructive. The Pardoner plays on the technical meanings of *substance* and *accident*, but with the suggestion also that gluttony changes the abiding and worthwhile into something fleeting and worthless. Drunkenness, a subdivision of gluttony, is "verray sepulture / Of mannes wit and his discrecioun" (558-59), a waste of human faculties. In the second division of the sermon, "hasardrye" is portrayed as "wast also / Of catel and of time" (593-94). And oaths in the third division of the sermon are a waste of speech: "But idel sweryng is a cursednesse" (638).

The whole first part of the tale harks back to the many misdirected sermons in the preceding group of tales. In those tales the sermons were a waste, in a sense, because the claims of experience overrode the claims of authority. The first part of the Pardoner's sermon is a waste in a deeper sense, however. The rioters in the exemplum do not hear it, and the one who delivers it does not believe it or even pretend to. The moralizing of the Pardoner's sermon is mirrored within the exemplum by the Old Man's rebuke to the three rioters, which has no effect on them. The world-view of the Pardoner's tale "accounts for" the inefficacy of *auctoritee*, but on different grounds from the tales of the preceding group. Both on the level of the fiction (the exemplum) and on the level of the "real world" (of the pilgrimage), authority fails not because experience is more valuable, but because evil is triumphant—not because people are fools, but because they are knaves.

Ironically, the way in which speech is *not* wasted is evident in the fact that the tale moves us and terrifies us. The world of the tale is like a machine running down, a clockwork that is programmed to destroy itself. The only thing admirable about the machine is its efficiency in purging the earth of life. If I may venture a paradox, the Pardoner's tale is frightening because of its economy of waste. The rioters are incapable of sticking to any purpose for long, but every foolish decision brings them closer to destruction. The world cooperates with them. The Old Man directs them to death. The "feend, oure enemy" (844) teaches the youngest rioter the strategem of the poison. In an interesting parallel to the Physician's tale, the Pardoner points out that the source of the evil is the depravity of the rioter. He first has to have the will to take all the treasure, and the "feend" only shows the way—just as Appius had first to lust for Virginia, before the "feend into his herte ran." We cannot, in other words, "explain" human evil by hypothesizing devils that possess men and give them evil desires. The desires are from the human heart; the devils only provide the means. The apothecary, too, seems almost devilish in the tale. He seems to know exactly why the young rioter wants the poison, and to be perfectly willing to cooperate in the murder—out of no conceivable motive:

> In al this world ther is no creature,
> That eten or dronken hath of this confiture
> Noght but the montance of a corn of whete,
> That he ne shal his lif anon forlete.   (861-64)

Precisely the terrifying thing about the Pardoner's tale is this delicately maintained balance between the supernaturally horrible and the every-day. To a certain extent—and this observation will be important in my discussion of fragment VII—the maintaining of the balance is a linguistic matter, a matter of word-play. If we read the apothecary's speech as I do, we hear a speech that on its everyday level could be spoken by an innocent druggist to advertise his rat-poison. But on another level, we hear a devilish irony, an unmotivated willingness to cooperate in evil. Similarly, the word *death* undergoes several transmutations in the tale. We hear of a "privee theef men clepeth Deeth" (675), and we wonder at first whether there is actually going to be a terrifying character in the tale named Death, in the mode of a morality play. The rioters' drunken search for Death is then made to seem comic, an instance of everyday folly. When this Death turns out to be bushels of gold florins, we seem to descend from the supernatural to the natural. And yet, the gold is "the death of" the rioters, figuratively speaking. So the everyday world takes on a grim, supernatural significance.

The best example in the tale of this mysterious balancing between supernatural and everyday is, of course, the figure of the Old Man, who has been called everything from the Wandering Jew to the Mercy of God.[19] Like the apothecary, the Old Man exists on two levels. He seems at once mysterious and supernatural, on the one hand, and on the other a realistic portrayal of an old man. Without attempting to settle specifically what the Old Man "represents," I would remark that in his former aspect he suggests the mystery and hostile unintelligibility of the world of the tale. Evil is not confined to the tavern and the human world, but is somehow involved at the core of the universe. But in his aspect as simply an old man, the character represents the alternative to dying young:

> Ne Deeth, allas! ne wol nat han my lyf.
> Thus walke I, lyk a restelees kaityf,
> And on the ground, which is my moodres gate,
> I knokke with my staf, bothe erly and late,
> And seye, "Leeve mooder, leet me in!
> Lo how I vanysshe, flessh, and blood, and skyn!
> Allas! whan shul my bones been at reste?" (727-33)

This is not a seductive picture of the joys of old age. Death is, of course, the exemplary human problem of evil. Not dying, the Old Man suggests, is as bad or worse. What is left is a dilemma, a problem that will not be gotten over. The fairy tales of the preceding group have neglected to recognize that the value of experience is not sufficient for what we really want it for—to overcome the problem of evil. Experience itself, as for the Old Man, eventually becomes meaningless suffering. The old woman in the Wife's tale, who was also wise and who also rebuked the young for despising the old, was able to save the young knight because she herself was not subject to time and decay. The Old Man in the Pardoner's tale can give only the directions that he knows will destroy the rioters, because he himself is the prisoner of experience. Perhaps the most poignant line in the tale is his declaration that "I moot go thider as I have to go" (749). In the Pardoner's tale, *The Canterbury Tales* as a whole finally comes directly to grips with the darkest side of human experience, in a vision not softened by time, distance, or fictionality. The Pardoner casts his shadow on the rest of the work.

CHAPTER SEVEN

Fragment VII:
The Problem of Language

Like fragments III-V, fragment VII seems to be sustained in part by dramatic interaction, as Kittredge early pointed out. But perhaps the most important critical insight into this group is the observation, made by various critics in various ways, that all the tales have something to do with *literature*.[1] I read the fragment as a reaction to the dark vision of the Pardoner's tale. Until the Nun's Priest's tale, the fragment is a series of attempts, all more or less weak and ineffective, to deal with the problem of evil in a literary way—by telling stories. The paradigm for the Middle Ages is perhaps the saint's life, in which we are shown how the sufferings of a saint are transmuted into glory. That is the Prioress' tactic. The paradigm for the classical world is the tragedy, an attempt to transmute human suffering into an edifying spectacle. That tactic, with some specifically medieval adaptations, is the Monk's. But there are other ways to deal with the problem of evil in a literary fashion. The Shipman's fabliau is a parodic inversion of the Pardoner's tale—a plot involving broken oaths and motives of greed ends happily, because of linguistic manipulation of the social world. "Chaucer's" tales are, first, a hilariously unsuccessful attempt to distract us from the problem of evil; and second, an allegorical rationalization of the proper human attitude toward that problem. And so the series goes, until the whole enterprise explodes in the mockery of the Nun's Priest's tale. By making fun of everything that has gone before it, the Nun's Priest's tale calls into question first the attempt to deal linguistically with the problem of evil—to explain it away, narrate it away, or drown it in the *solaas* of literature. But the tale also by implication calls into question the whole literary enterprise. If literature cannot deal adequately with the fundamental human problem, what good is it? And so ironically, in a move of the subtlety we expect of Chaucer, the "best" tale, the very tale whose world-view is perhaps the most satisfactory of all, is the tale that most calls into question the whole enterprise that author and reader embarked on with the first line of the General Prologue. In the tales that follow the Nun's Priest's tale the work never quite recovers from this questioning of the literary enterprise. Except for the Parson's tale, which has its own strictly limited, orthodox vision, all the rest of the tales and the Retractation itself question the validity of language as a tool of knowledge and as a way of dealing with the human and superhuman worlds. I think the Nun's Priest's tale thus represents a crucial point in a thematic reading of *The Canterbury Tales*, an explosion of some of the illusions of fiction, a turning of attention away from the world mirrored by language and toward that process of mirroring itself.

The Shipman's Tale

The Shipman's tale has sometimes been compared[2] or contrasted[3] with the Merchant's tale, and the critical controversy about the tale centers on the question of whether it is basically "jolly" or whether it means to denounce the merchant who is duped by his wife and the monk.[4] I place the Shipman's tale at the head of a group of tales that attempt to respond to the Pardoner's vision of evil. The Shipman's tale then appears a kind of ironic inversion of the Pardoner's tale, even a sort of parody, which adopts a world-view not nearly so dark as that of the Pardoner's tale. Furthermore, the Shipman's tale represents a specifically *linguistic* cure for the problem of evil. Evil in the social context—and that is the only context of the Shipman's tale—can be dealt with effectively through the medium of language. Or so the world-view of the tale implies.

Whereas the Pardoner's tale shows us a world of wasting, the Shipman's tale shows us a world of accumulating. The rioters publicly disperse their goods, and they want the florins so that they can continue to waste. The merchant in the Shipman's tale, however, is full of anxiety ("curious bisynesse"—225) about his profits and is pedantic about his wife's responsibility to "Keep bet my good" (432). The beginning lines imply that this merchant hates waste: he hates to buy clothes for wives, "But thynketh it is wasted and ylost" (16-17). And before leaving for Flanders, he tells his wife, "for to kepe oure good be curious" (243). We get two very clear images of the merchant. One of them is the picture of him in bed with his wife at the end of the tale. But the other is the picture of him in his counting-house at the beginning:

> His bookes and his bagges many oon
> He leith biforn hym on his countyng-bord.
> Ful riche was his tresor and his hord,
> For which ful faste his countour-dore he shette.... (82-85)

The Merchant's wife likes to spend (5), and in this she resembles the monk (43). But she cannot manage to spend more than the merchant makes. At the end of the story, the merchant has made a large profit (365 ff.), and, as his wife points out, even the hundred franks have been spent "on myn array, / And nat on wast" (418-19).

But the merchant is not a hoarder. He is known for his "largesse" (22), and his life actually seems to move between the two poles of bed and counting-board. Money-making seems to give the merchant sexual vigor: "And al that nyght in myrthe they bisette; / For he was riche and cleerly out of dette" (375-76).[5] And though the image of the merchant in his counting-house is extraordinarily powerful, it is offset by the extraordinary number of times we see him indulging himself in "pleye." There are references in lines 59, 73, 117 (where his wife falsely accuses him of "sory pley" in bed), 297, 337, 381, and 422. The merchant seems at least as concerned with amusing himself as he does with accumulating money. Indeed, "pleyyng" seems to be the basis of his relationship with the monk, since the word seems to occur where the merchant seeks the monk's companionship. The other characters in the story, too, like to play—several times, the characters are compared to birds, suggesting a kind of carefree indulgence in pleasure (38, 51, 209, 369).[6] In short, the world of the Shipman's tale is an inversion of the Pardoner's world. In the world of the Pardoner's tale, the rioters act with complete irresponsibility, and they encounter a universe that strikes them down pitilessly and inexorably. In the Shipman's tale, the merchant acts responsibly, and his reward is that he can then be carefree for a time. No one but a fool is carefree in the Pardoner's world. Even the rioters, between the anger of the dice-game and the blustering at Death and the worry about the treasure and the murders, do not get the benefits of their irresponsibility.

Another way the Shipman's tale seems a parodic inversion of the Pardoner's tale is in the pattern of oaths and betrayals. Like the three rioters, the merchant and the monk swear brotherhood:

> Thus been they knyt with eterne alliaunce,
> And ech of hem gan oother for t'assure
> Of bretherhede, whil that hir lyf may dure.   (40-42)
>   (compare lines 702 ff. of the Pardoner's tale)

Monk and wife swear oaths of secrecy (131 ff.; compare 819 ff. of the Pardoner's tale). The monk swears to lend the wife the money (198-201). In the background, of course, is always the wife's marriage-vow to the merchant. Thus the three characters are connected in a system of mutual obligation, voluntarily entered into, like the rioters in the Pardoner's tale. And like the rioters in the Pardoner's tale, the characters set about betraying each other. The wife betrays the merchant by boldly taking the first steps that lead to adultery. Then, in an ironic reversal corresponding to the young rioter's poisoning the bottles, the monk, having betrayed the merchant, betrays the wife as well by telling the merchant that he has "repaid" the hundred franks.

But in a dénouement strikingly different from that of the Pardoner's tale, everything turns out all right.[7] The Shipman's tale shows us that betrayals do not necessarily have grim consequences, that life is rarely as stark as it is portrayed to be in the exemplum of the rioters, and that in fact it is foolish to think that human beings are always wrestling with ultimate evil in their everyday lives.

Another elegant symmetry between the two tales further reinforces the contrast. Money in the Pardoner's tale becomes symbolic of the rioters' wasting and of death that is the ultimate waste. Money in the Shipman's tale, however, becomes symbolic of, almost equivalent to, sex.[8] In the Pardoner's tale the goods of the world lead inexorably to death; in the Shipman's tale, to pleasure. But there is a deeper contrast here that I think goes to the heart of the difference between the two tales. That contrast has to do with the attitudes toward language in the tales. The identification of money with death in the Pardoner's tale is a matter of word-play—that is, the florins are "the death of" the rioters. But it is in no sense *just* word-play. The structure of the universe in the Pardoner's tale is such that the word-play corresponds to, points to, a deeper reality. Allegory is a valid mode of perception in the Pardoner's tale, and, indeed, the rioters are destroyed because they cannot penetrate the Old Man's verbal allegory. There is something sinister and hidden in the universe, which reveals itself in the verbal identification of money with death.

In the Shipman's tale, the resolution depends upon a different kind of word-play. Critics have pointed out the importance of the wife's pun on *taille* (echoed in the last line of the tale) in composing the differences between her and her husband.[9] And David H. Abraham offers an ingenious study of another possible pun on *cosyn/cosynage* to show that the whole structure of the Shipman's tale is pun-like in that it is "based upon a recognition and balancing of two possible perspectives of the same situation—the monk-wife-merchant triangle."[10] In any case, the tale depends crucially upon the manipulation of language by the characters. The attitude toward language in the tale is quite different from that in the Pardoner's tale. The money in the Pardoner's tale is always death, just as the Old Man says. But the hundred franks in the Shipman's tale change their aspect radically, depending on what they are called. When the monk asks the merchant for the money, it is a *loan*:

> O thyng, er that ye goon, if it may be,
> I wolde prey yow; for to lene me
> An hundred frankes. (269-71)

When the monk and the wife discuss the hundred franks, on the other hand, the money becomes quite clearly *payment* for services rendered:

> This faire wyf acorded with daun John
> That for thise hundred frankes he sholde al nyght
> Have hire in his armes bolt upright;
> And this acord parfourned was in dede. (314-17)

Finally, when the wife explains to the merchant about the hundred franks, the money through her inventiveness suddenly becomes a *gift*:

> For, God it woot, I wende, withouten doute,
> That he hadde yeve it me bycause of yow,
> To doon therwith myn honour and my prow. (406-08)

The hundred franks go through so many metamorphoses in the tale that they are as hard to keep one's eye on as the pea in a shell-game, almost a phantom hundred franks like the phantom dollars in our checking accounts.

The point is that the world of the tale works, and everybody ends happily, because the actual hundred franks are this kind of phantom entity that can put on different aspects depending upon what people call it. Unlike the real, hard, beautiful florins of the Pardoner's tale, the hundred franks have a kind of ghostliness about them, and can become real only when people call them something. The money is like a natural phenomenon in the Pardoner's tale. It is described in highly concrete terms: "floryns fyne of gold ycoyned rounde / Wel ny an eighte busshels" (770-71). The rioters admire its physical beauty: "ech of hem so glad was of that sighte, / For that the floryns been so faire and brighte" (773-74). The hundred franks in the Shipman's tale, though, are a cultural phenomenon. Because people can be gotten to agree on words to call things, reality comes under linguistic control. Allegory is not valid in the same way it is in the Pardoner's tale, for there is in a sense no hard, extralinguistic reality for a double meaning to reveal. Reality is culturally determined, and it is a good thing that that is so; for otherwise, all sorts of violence and disharmony would result. We have, in short, a kind of linguistic solution to the problem of evil, a world-view that sees "glossing over" not as destructive, but as the essential cultural activity.

And that brings us to the problem with the Shipman's tale, the slightly repellent coolness we feel in it that Owen has described as its "respectable surfaces"[11] and Donaldson has called its "smooth, glassy

90

surface" unscratched by emotion.[12] Ruggiers, I think, has the clearest statement, when he calls the tale a "social comedy."[13] The crucial point is the *social* nature of the tale, the insistence that reality is social and is therefore under linguistic control. Ruggiers is perhaps guilty of an ethnic slur when he says that "the tale, while brilliant, is either too Gallic or wanting in humanity" (p. 88). But his statement strikes a responsive chord in these latter days of French structuralism, which in its insistence on the determinism of cultural structures abolishes the notion of the subject and drives the individual human being out of his place as the center of creative consciousness. It is precisely that tendency, that paradoxical coolness toward humanity arising from fascination with the cultural manifestations that define humanity, that we object to in the Shipman's tale. The opposite error, of course, is sentimentality, and that is the error into which the Prioress' tale falls.

The Prioress' Tale

The problem in the Prioress' tale is the Jews.[14] But the goal of a critical enterprise is not historical knowledge about whether or in what sense Chaucer was anti-Semitic (although such knowledge might help us in a critical enterprise). The goal of a critical enterprise is the articulation of meaning—in this case, an articulation of the function of what is usually taken as the anti-Semitism in the tale. Critics articulate the Jews one way if the tale is taken as a dramatic speech portraying the Prioress, and another way if it is taken as portraying a self-consistent world-view competing for interest with the other world-views in *The Canterbury Tales*.

In fact, we need not talk about bigotry at all in a thematic reading of the Prioress' tale. Alfred David points out that the Jews are after all more like fairy-tale monsters than human beings, and the tale is a "children's story told with a childlike fantasy."[15] Bigotry seizes on some particular, carefully selected aspect of experience to hate. The hatreds of childhood, like its affections, are extreme but not selective. The important point in David's analysis, as it seems to me, is the suggestion that the extreme emotion expended on the Jews is of a piece with the extreme emotion expended on the "litel clergeon." We have, not bigotry, but sentimentality.[16]

Sentimentality seizes on everything that comes its way and plunges it into a bath of emotion. Thus, the Prioress' tale is an appropriate contrast to the emotionless Shipman's tale. As, indeed, the monk who is "an hooly man, / As monkes been—or elles oghte be" (642-43) is an explicit contrast to the calculating monk in the Shipman's tale. This pious monk exhibits the exemplary reaction to the martyrdom: "His salte teeris trikled doun as reyn, / And gruf he fil al plat upon the grounde" (674-75). Everything in the Prioress' tale is rhetorically milked for the maximum emotional effect, and it is already the story of a child-martyr, a genre that when appropriately adapted still brings tears even in Protestant congregations. But sentimentality is not just emotion—it is indulging in the appropriate emotion, the expected emotion. Everyone is supposed to love children, especially pious children, and to be sorry when they die.

> ... in a tombe of marbul stones cleere
> Enclosen they his litel body sweete.
> Ther he is now, God leve us for to meete!   (681-83)

That the Prioress plans to draw on stock responses is made clear by her prologue, which depends heavily on Scripture and on the liturgy. That her assessment of her audience is accurate is indicated by the first lines of the prologue to *Sir Thopas*: "Whan seyd was al this miracle, every man / As sobre was that wonder was to se" (691-92). The blasts against the Jews are just the other side of the same coin, excessive emotionalism drawing on stock responses. *Jews* need not have been the villains of this piece. Any evil person would have done as well, and would have been subjected to as much vituperation.

Whittock has pointed out the affinities between the Prioress' tale and the Physician's tale: "Both treat of a plot by wicked people directed at an innocent and young person, and both show the wicked being found out. In *The Physician's Tale* the young girl is killed by her father to prevent her degradation. In *The Prioress's Tale* the child is murdered and his body degraded... but the innocent spirit is unquenched."[17] The insight is important, I think, because it indicates where the Prioress' tale fits in the structure of *The Canterbury Tales*. The tale is an attempt to resolve the problem of irremediable evil, the problem posed by fragment VI and answered in one way, though unacceptably from an orthodox Christian view, in the Shipman's tale.

Furthermore, the Prioress' tale is an attempt to resolve the problem linguistically. The tale begins with a prayer in which the Prioress says that her intent is to praise Christ and the Virgin (460-61), and asks for divine aid (481-87). The "litel clergeon" is learning to sing a song in Mary's praise as well, and the song is not only the occasion of his martyrdom and the instrument that brings his murderers to justice; it is also transmuted into a heavenly song in the crucial stanza of the poem where the Prioress argues explicitly that apparent earthly evil really works for good:

> O martir, sowded to virginitee,
> Now maystow syngen, folwynge evere in oon
> The white Lamb celestial—quod she—
> Of which the grete evaungelist, Seint John,
> In Pathmos wroot, which seith that they that goon
> Biforn this Lamb, and synge a song al newe,
> That nevere, flesshly, wommen they ne knewe.   (579-85)

Not only is the child fortunate to have been killed, but he is fortunate to have died young so that he is still a virgin. The language of praise thus becomes a redemption of apparent evil; also, the language of revelation, what "Seint John" wrote, becomes a justification of earthly experience and provides a context in which evil appears clearly as the nothingness, the mere absence of good, that is its true nature. The "greyn" on the child's tongue is at once life and praise—as long as the "greyn" is there, he remains alive and must sing the *Alma redemptoris*. Clearly the child's understanding of the hymn is emotional rather than intellectual—he never knows what it says, exactly; he knows only that it is in praise of Mary (523, 531 ff.). The intellectual understanding, obviously, is not important. The emotional response is what counts, both for the child and for the world-view of the tale in general. In the world-view of the tale, the solution to the problem of evil is to drown it in the deep emotional response called forth by and issuing in the language of praise. This emotional response is itself a revelation of the "true" nature of the universe created by a benevolent God. Sorrow and suffering are ultimately good, if for no other reason, because they touch the deepest springs of human nature and call forth the affective response to experience.

But as Whittock points out, the "quod she" (581) in the middle of the crucial stanza of the poem is like a reserving of judgment,[18] almost a dash of cold water. "Or so she said"—and the reservation might apply to the whole of the tale when it is considered in the cool light of intellect. Ultimately, pathos is not an answer to the problem of evil. At best, it is a temporary stay, and we can hold off the problem of evil only so long as we can actually sustain that odd mood in which we enjoy our pity, drowning our critical faculties in our affective response.

Sir Thopas and the Tale of Melibee

Chaucer's tales belong together as two sides of a coin. More than any others, these tales seem to resist the efforts of modern criticism. It is almost as though Chaucer, like some poets of our own day, deliberately set out to write works that would baffle methods of criticism. *Sir Thopas* is a joke that vanishes in the explaining.[19] And though critics have been able to find the *Melibeus* sententious,[20] philosophically and theologically "true,"[21] and appropriate to the dramatic structure of *The Canterbury Tales*[22] or to Chaucer's own personal milieu,[23] nobody with a normal threshold of boredom has been able to find it interesting.

Allen and Moritz note that these two tales "attempt to isolate sentence from solace, and present each separately."[24] That is, in a storytelling contest where the object is to present tales of most *sentence* and of most *solaas*, Chaucer, the author of the whole fiction, gives himself in the *Thopas* the tale with the least *sentence*, and in the *Melibeus* the tale with the least *solaas*. That is the same as saying that these tales, of all those in the Canterbury collection, are the most *literary* in the pejorative sense. In these tales Chaucer creates worlds that seem nearly independent of anything outside the text itself. Here, as nowhere else in *The Canterbury Tales*, there is, as Jacques Derrida says, nothing outside the text. Derrida, of course, would say that this is true of all texts. But I want to argue that Chaucer is making this the particular point of *these* two tales.

In the first place, the plot of these two tales is not a source of interest. But usually in *The Canterbury Tales*, plot is a major source of interest. The concept of *plot* implies a structure of events in cause-and-effect sequence, presented as independent of the telling of them, events which can therefore be told about in different ways. But there *is* no story in this sense either in *Sir Thopas* or in the *Tale of Melibee*. Manner is everything, matter is nothing. Sir Thopas does not perform actions, but random motion. He falls in love with the elf-queen he has never seen and whose very existence he has no reason to believe in; the giant distracts him from that quest; he arms himself apparently to fight the giant, but when the Host interrupts the second fit, there is every indication that the giant has slipped out of Sir Thopas' mind and the narrator's as well. The transitions in the tale do not represent causal links between events, but random occurrences: "And so bifel upon a day" (748); "Til that ther cam a greet geaunt" (807); "Til on a day—" (918). The *Melibeus* has a plot, on the "literal" level of the allegory, but the events of that literal level are taken up into the allegorical level in such a way as to show that they do not mean what they appear to mean, and that their literal significance is minimal compared to the intellectual grasping of them that results from allegorical interpretation. Who would have believed that the surgeons, physicians, and lawyers actually meant what Prudence says they do? And who would believe that a man's enemies would submit to him as meekly as Melibeus' do, unless the world being depicted is the purely intelligible rational world, and not the material world of event? In a different sense than with *Sir Thopas*, manner is all and matter nothing. What is important is not the events, but how one understands them.

As spoof and allegory, respectively, *Sir Thopas* and the *Tale of Melibee* are already derivative literary forms.[25] Spoof, as a specifically literary joke, does not necessarily depend upon specific knowledge of specific works that are parodied. We would know that *Sir Thopas* is funny even if we did not know any other romances. But the form exploits the potential for absurdity inherent in the very notion of literary form itself. Explicit allegory is derivative in that it joins two "stories," the story of the literal level and the story of the allegorical level, where the second story is a given, a pre-existing system of doctrine to be exposited. But the allegory consists in the joining itself, which happens only in the text—just as the self-parody of spoof occurs only in the text. Both of these literary forms, then, are inherently self-referential or reflexive, and therefore we have a hard time talking about them once we have seen the joke or located the explicit moral of the allegory.

It is interesting that Chaucer presents himself as adopting two different stances toward the two works. He intimates to the Host that he has memorized *Sir Thopas* and is reciting it slavishly (lines 707-09). In the case of the *Melibeus*, however, Chaucer presents himself as tampering with the source, adding more proverbs or sententious remarks to the version of the tale with which his audience might be familiar (lines 953-64).[26] And of course what makes the *Melibeus* so boring is the vast weight of proverbs and sententiousness. Chaucer is calling attention to the two possible responses of the medieval author to his source-material: slavishly pass it on, or reshape it.[27] The decision the author has to make is not how to apply the stories to his social milieu or his personal experience, but what changes, if any, are to be made in the *text*.

Since *Sir Thopas* and the *Tale of Melibee* seem to be presented as specifically literary objects for which there is nothing outside the text, the joke is on the audience, if we believe that language can deal with the problem of evil.[28] *Sir Thopas* follows the Prioress' tale, in which the Prioress attempts to resolve the problem of evil, or, perhaps more accurately, dissolve it in a bath of emotion. *Sir Thopas*, too, represents a kind of distraction from the problems of human existence, an escapism of the shallowest kind, in juxtaposition with which the Prioress' tale appears almost profound but still unsatisfactory. The point of the juxtaposition seems to be that the two tales differ in degree and not in kind.[29] The modern phenomenon that seems to me closest to *Sir Thopas* is the television situation-comedy, which at its worst becomes a self-parody, a negative comment on the medium itself, and an implicit criticism of the whole society that spawned it. To the extent that we can continue to be distracted from human problems by literature like *Sir Thopas*, we have serious moral problems or, at best, seriously warped instincts. *Sir Thopas* is amusing for a while, but once we get the point, it is exactly what Harry Bailly calls it: "drasty speche" (923). Whatever else we might say about Bailly's sophistication as a literary critic, it is to his credit that he has the sense to change the channel.

The *Tale of Melibeus* attempts to deal with the problem of evil by intellectualizing, by transporting us to an allegorical world that is purely rational and intelligible and therefore has very little resemblance to the world we all live in—the world of matter, of contingency, and of incomprehensible events. The crucial passage in the tale is Prudence's explanation of Melibeus' sufferings, which will bear quoting at some length:

> Now, sire, if men wolde axe me why that God suffred men to do yow this vileynye, certes, I kan nat wel answere, as for no sooth-fastnesse. For th'apostle seith that 'the sciences and the juggmentz of oure Lord God almyghty been ful depe; ther may no man comprehende ne serchen hem suffisantly.' Nathelees, by certeyne presumpciouns and conjectynges, I holde and bileeve that God, which that is ful of justice and of rightwisnesse, hath suffred this bityde by juste cause resonable.
>
> Thy name is Melibee, this is to seyn, 'a man that drynketh hony.' Thou has ydronke so muchel hony of sweete temporeel richesses, and delices and honours of this world, that thou art dronken, and has forgeten Jhesu Crist thy creatour. (1405-12)

Prudence's solution to the problem of evil is specifically rational. Though she admits that God's providence is ultimately unsearchable, nevertheless it sometimes seems comprehensible by "certeyne presumpciouns and conjectynges." Prudence, of course, in her allegorical meaning, is the rational faculty which, while it is not alone sufficient to save man, is very helpful in most situations where one has to decide how to live in the world. Her intellectualism is a strong contrast to the Prioress' emotionalism, not to mention the "litel clergeon's" lack of prudence in flaunting his piety in the face of the evil Jews every day. But Prudence's solution is also specifically linguistic. Melibeus is to understand his suffering, she asserts, through meditating upon his *name*. In a deep sense, what has happened to Melibeus in the story has happened *because* he is called what he is. The qualities, and especially the names, of entities in the world, both human and non-human, become comprehensible only by being related to the allegorical level of the story. Even the words of the doctors and lawyers, which Prudence accepts as good counsel, do not mean what they say on the literal level. But they are redeemed by allegorical interpretation. Language gives us the key to the problem of evil—once we strip off the husk and penetrate to the allegorical kernel.

But of course, in the *Melibeus* as in all explicit allegory, the allegory controls the event. The enemies throw themselves on Melibeus' mercy not because people would behave that way, but because an allegorical point is being made. Melibeus and Prudence and Sophie have their names not because there was some family with those names, but because those names are needed to make the allegory comprehensible. The linguistic solution to the problem of evil is smuggled in, as it were, in the literary form itself. We have a self-referential, purely intelligible, rational world, which has about as much relation to the problem of evil in real life as Euclid's *Elements* does. "Presuming" or "conjecturing" the problem of evil out of existence does not remove it from experience, and the *Melibeus* by directly discussing the problem after the escapism of *Sir Thopas* only sharpens the issue that the Prioress' tale attempted to blur with tears.

The Monk's Tale

The Monk's tale is a failure in the world of the pilgrimage—as the Knight's interruption indicates—and a failure at doing what tragedy is supposed to do. The literate Monk opts for a literary attempt to deal with the problem of evil, an attempt to transmute suffering into art. Whether or not the Monk's tale presents a philosophically sound, Boethian statement about Fortune,[30] it fails first on the level where it invites us to judge it, namely as literary art. Every reader of the tale has felt this failure,[31] and I think all the more so because the Monk's tale follows another consciously literary performance. The Monk admits the existence of incomprehensible events and apparent evil, and attempts to deal with the problem by removing the events from the audience through the aesthetic distancing of tragedy.

I do not find a developing conception of Fortune in the tale,[32] but I can agree that Fortune plays different roles in the different tragedies.[33] In some of the tragedies God directly brings about the fall; in others Fortune brings about the fall, acting as God's agent; and in others God seems to play little part. In some of the tragedies, the fall is merited because of some sin or folly of the protagonist; in others, the protagonist's suffering seems undeserved. Lucifer falls "for his synne" (2002), not through Fortune (2001) but presumably through God. Adam falls "for mysgovernaunce" (2012), again presumably through God's direct action (2013). Sampson falls through the betrayal of his wife, because of his own human folly in telling her his secrets (2021, 2053, 2062-65, 2092). Hercules falls either through Dianira's poisoning of the shirt, or through

97

Nessus' deception—the Monk refuses to say (2127-29); but his fall, unmerited through any sin on his part, is ultimately blamed on Fortune (2135 ff.). Nebuchadnezzar falls through God's direct action (2168), as a result of his pride (2159, 2167); Balthasar his son falls also through pride (2186, 2188, 2223), and by God's acting (2225, 2231) through Fortune (2189, 2241 ff.). Zenobia seems not to deserve her fall, which is attributed solely to Fortune (2347-50, 2367-69); and the same in general is true of the rest of the "modern instances"—Peter of Spain (2376), Peter of Cyprus (2397), Barnabo of Lombardy (2401), and Ugolino (2413, 2445, 2457). Nero mightily deserves death for his vices and crimes, and his fall is attributed to Fortune (2478, 2519-26, 2550). Holofernes, guilty of "heigh presumpcioun" (2555), is brought down by Fortune (2556). Antiochus, proud and "venymus" (2577), is struck down by God (2599), who is this case works *against* Fortune (2583). Alexander, worthy and noble, is destroyed by Fortune (2661, 2669), and the same is true of Julius Caesar (2678, 2723-26) and, within Caesar's story, of Pompey (2687-94). Finally, Croesus' pride (2729, 2741) is brought low by Fortune (2737).

I cite all these instances to demonstrate that it is difficult to find a pattern here, either philosophical or literary. The Ellesmere manuscript places the "modern instances" (the Peters through Ugolino) at the end of the tale, an order rejected by Robinson's edition, among others. There are arguments for restoring this order,[34] in spite of the apparent reference in line 2782 of the prologue of the Nun's Priest's tale to the last line of Croesus' tragedy. The Ellesmere order does have the advantage of concluding with the group of tragedies where the suffering is clearly unmerited and where it is clearest, as William C. Strange puts it, that "Neither God's justice nor the world's order is in evidence, and when faced with events that are so close in time, some explanations that are doctrinally correct become emotionally inadequate or difficult."[35] Ruggiers argues that the Monk's tale is anomalous in Chaucer's poetry, because Chaucer usually provides "either a redemptive close or a justification of law and morality suited to an audience's needs."[36] In my reading, the anomalousness of the Monk's tale is precisely the point. Neither as philosophical justification of apparent evil, nor, especially, as literary transmutation of suffering into art does the Monk's tale serve the needs of the fictive pilgrims, or our needs.

The Nun's Priest's Tale

After all of the effort of recent decades to decide what the theme of the Nun's Priest's tale "really" is,[37] and all of the attempts to account for the tale on dramatic grounds as a reply to the Monk, to the Prioress, or to other pilgrims,[38] I think the most insightful comment is still that of E. Talbot Donaldson. Donaldson suggests that the point of the tale is to be found in the "enormous rhetorical elaboration of the telling," where rhetoric is "regarded as the inadequate defense that mankind erects against an inscrutable reality.... In short, the fruit of the Nun's Priest's Tale is its chaff."[39]

Along these same lines, John M. Fyler has said that in the tale "the comic human resources of language and rhetoric try on their own to reintegrate the disordered, unresolved conflicts of the *Canterbury Tales*."[40] Fyler and others have remarked the constant shifting of perspective in the tale, as one after another philosophical and rhetorical position is assumed, only to be puffed away as the reader is made to recognize the limitations of all points of view.[41] There is, then, a considerable body of critical opinion that regards the Nun's Priest's tale pretty much as my reading of *The Canterbury Tales* would lead one to expect. The tale laughs into tatters the serious pretensions of the preceding tales in the fragment to deal with the problem of evil, and it does so largely by laughing at the inadequacy of rhetoric, of language, to confront this problem. I have tried to show how the preceding tales in the fragment attempt various kinds of linguistic or rhetorical or literary solutions to the problem of evil. Now, the Nun's Priest's tale shows the folly of such attempts. The Nun's Priest's tale in the process seriously calls into question the whole literary enterprise, the whole of *The Canterbury Tales*, and the whole of the life of the poet. Ironically, in the jolliest of his tales Chaucer poses the most searching and painful question for authors and readers of literature —the question of the validity of language itself as a way of knowing.

Before discussing this ultimate question, however, I should like to show in more detail how the Nun's Priest's tale calls into question the attempts of the preceding tales. The Nun's Priest's tale seems to work, in particular, by showing that the rhetorical stances adopted in the other tales are self-contradictory, that at the heart of every attempt to deal with or cover over the problem of evil by rhetoric there is a fundamental conflict. I shall argue this point by looking at some of the famous passages in the Nun's Priest's tale and relating them to the strategies of the other tales in the fragment.

First, let us consider Chauntecleer's "mistranslation":

> For al so siker as *In principio,*
> *Mulier est hominis confusio,*—
> Madame, the sentence of this Latyn is,
> 'Womman is mannes joye and al his blis.' (3163-66)

Whether Chauntecleer is deliberately mistranslating and thus having a joke on Pertelote, or whether he is unaware of the mistranslation and is therefore himself the butt of the joke,[42] we have here a manipulation of language for social purposes that is, to my mind at least, reminiscent of the punning in the Shipman's tale. The merchant's wife puns on *taille* to say something that will make her husband happy, and at the same time to present the unpleasant fact that he will have to extend her credit. Similarly, Chauntecleer appeases Pertelote, taking the sting out of his 200-line demonstration of her intellectual inferiority, and at the same time (wittingly or unwittingly) he calls her exactly the unflattering name she deserves—the source of his confusion, on several levels. The joke implies that we can separate the thing the word stands for from the use to which the word is put in the social situation, just as the physical hundred franks in the Shipman's tale could assume entirely different sorts of reality, depending upon what word was used for them. The difference between the two tales, however, is obvious—reality is considerably stubborner in the Nun's Priest's tale. In spite of his assertion that his "confusion" is his "bliss," Pertelote (the referent of both terms) remains a confusion for Chauntecleer. It is not so easy as it is in the Shipman's tale to manipulate reality linguistically. Reality depends upon something more fundamental than the social contract.

What Jill Mann calls the "basic intractability of human nature and human experience"[43] in the Nun's Priest's tale points up an apparent contradiction in the view of language adopted in the Shipman's tale. The question is whether words are real or unreal, whether they have an existence and power of their own, or whether they have only a secondary power and existence deriving from the entities they name. Are words merely obedient servants, as Humpty Dumpty would have it in *Through the Looking Glass*, which can mean anything we want them to mean? Or are they themselves powerful realities with fundamental connections to the being of the entities they name (as in the *Melibeus*), so that we abuse them at our peril? The Shipman's tale wants it both ways. On the one hand, words as creations of culture can be given any meaning the culture pleases—connections between words and things are arbitrary, and thus punning is possible; the "same" word can refer to a woman's sexual organs and to a tally stick. On the other hand, words are powerful shapers of social reality. If the wife can get the merchant to call the hundred franks a "gift" instead of a "payment," she can extract herself from a great deal of trouble. The contradiction never shows itself as long as we think the only reality is social. The relation between words and the entities they name is reciprocal, a developing relation of mutual determining. But as soon as one postulates a brute, intractable reality apart from words, as happens in the Nun's Priest's tale, the contradiction becomes painfully obvious. As long as there is nothing outside the culture, words can seem without contradiction to be both counters and powers. But if there is something beyond or beneath the cultural, then we have to doubt our ability to get linguistic control of the problem of evil by punning it away or giving it euphemistic names.

The Nun's Priest's tale seems to allude directly to the Prioress' tale in lines 3050 ff., where Chauntecleer temporarily gets distracted from the main thread of his argument and offers a "conclusion" only peripherally related to his thesis that "dremes been to drede" (3063). Chauntecleer's "conclusion" is, of course, the same sententious remark the Prioress offers in line 576 of her tale, "Mordre wol out, certeyn." Chauntecleer says,

> O blisful God, that art so just and trewe,
> Lo, how that thou biwreyest mordre alway!
> Mordre wol out, that se we day by day.
> Mordre is so wlatsom and abhomynable
> To God, that is so just and resonable,
> That he ne wol nat suffre it heled be,
> Though it abyde a yeer, or two, or thre.
> Mordre wol out, this my conclusioun.   (3050-57)

The passage mocks the rhetorical stance adopted by the Prioress' tale. In that tale, considered as an attempt to deal with the problem of evil, the matter of earthly justice or injustice is just as irrelevant as it is to the cock's thesis about dreams. That is, in the rhetorical stance that justifies earthly evil by pointing to heavenly reward, it does not matter whether murder is discovered on earth or not. The difference between the temporal perspective and the eternal perspective on such matters is emphasized in the line "Though it abyde a yeer, or two, or thre." From God's point of view—as defined, to be sure, by the rhetorical stance of the Prioress' tale itself—a year or two on the human scale does not make much difference. But it makes a great deal of difference from the human point of view. It is too painful to imagine the "litel clergeon" lying in the privy with his throat cut for a year or two or three. The passage in the Nun's Priest's tale sharply defines a contradiction in the rhetorical stance of the Prioress' tale, which wants to justify apparent evil by looking at things from the eternal perspective, and yet wants to deal with apparent evil in terms of contingent, time-bound, even disorderly and excessive human emotion.

The irony of the passage in the Nun's Priest's tale is palpable in the wrenching shifts of perspective in the following pairs of lines: "O blisful

101

God, that art so just and trewe, / Lo, how that thou biwreyest mordre alway!'' and "Mordre is so wlatsom and abhomynable / To God, that is so just and resonable.'' The obvious question is, if murder is so horrible to God, why does He permit it in the first place—in a nutshell, the problem of evil. The passage does not necessarily say that there is no answer to the question. But it does show that the rhetorical stance of the Prioress' tale, far from dealing effectively with the problem of evil, just sharpens it unendurably. From the eternal perspective, as Prudence also argues, God must seem "just and trewe,'' "just and resonable.'' And yet He permits murder, something He hates and uncovers in the temporal sphere, something "wlatsom and abhomynable'' from the human perspective. The point of the passage, and the deep point of the allusion to the Prioress' tale, is that the uncritical release of emotion does not resolve the problem of evil, but makes it worse. If emotion is released in praise of God and the Virgin, it is released equally in the hatred of murder and of the Jews. The affective response as manipulated in the rhetoric of the Prioress' tale is itself earthbound, time-bound, and so it cannot separate the eternal perspective from the temporal perspective. Though it might be possible to make the separation intellectually, the rhetorical stance adopted in the Prioress' tale sacrifices that possibility. There is thus a fundamental contradiction in the stance itself, which destroys its value for doing what it sets out to do.

Just as Chaucer's tales are the most "literary" in the pejorative sense, so the Nun's Priest's "answer" to them is the most telling objection to the literary enterprise. *Sir Thopas* pretends to be literature as pure *solaas*, pure distraction from the worrisome problem of evil and every other problem. An answer to that rhetorical stance comes in that extraordinarily ambiguous passage at the end of the Nun's Priest's tale:

> But ye that holden this tale a folye,
> As of a fox, or of a cok and hen,
> Taketh the moralite, goode men.
> For seint Paul seith that al that writen is,
> To oure doctrine it is ywrite, ywis;
> Taketh the fruyt, and lat the chaf be stille. (3438-43)

Modern criticism of the tale is *prima facie* evidence that it is far from clear what moral, if any, the Nun's Priest is alluding to.[44] The term *folye* here associates the Nun's Priest's tale with *Sir Thopas*, which is a "folly" in every sense. *Sir Thopas* does not succeed even as distraction, but the question it poses by its existence is whether literature *can* succeed as distraction. The rhetorical stance of *Sir Thopas* assumes that it can, and

102

that it can because literary *form* in itself has the potential for entertainment. *Sir Thopas* aspires to be pure form, pure entertainment.

If we regard this passage from the Nun's Priest's tale as a kind of answer to *Sir Thopas*, Jill Mann's reading of the passage seems most penetrating. The Nun's Priest does not offer some particular moral; "he can only offer St. Paul's guarantee that everything that has been written has a moral in it somewhere."[45] The tale itself might be as confused about its moral as modern critics are, in other words. The Nun's Priest, and Chaucer, predict exactly what will happen —what has happened— with this tale. Critics will be unable to agree on what the moral is, but they will nevertheless feel an irresistible impulse to formulate one. Why is this so? Precisely because the tale seems to have a form, but then the form is not apparently harmonious with the matter.[46]

We find this same discrepancy between form and content in *Sir Thopas*, of course. But if the Nun's Priest and St. Paul are correct, there must be a moral somewhere in *Sir Thopas*, too. What makes the *moralite* of a tale possible is its ability to be related to something else, to life as lived. What makes that relating possible is precisely the form of the tale. The tale must share its form with some form of life, at some level. St. Paul's statement, then, as interpreted (perhaps jokingly) by the Nun's Priest, is essentially that whatever has form is by that very fact capable of being related to life, and therefore capable of having *moralite*. But the point of *Sir Thopas* is just to *distract*, to avoid *moralite* and therefore to avoid being related to life as lived, through the exploitation of literary form. And this is the contradiction at the heart of the rhetorical stance that presents *Sir Thopas*. The paradox, of course, afflicts all literary works. Each literary work is in one sense a little world unto itself, and its form is precisely the principle of coherence at the heart of that world. But on the other hand, the literary work would be unintelligible if it could not be somehow connected to the "real world," to life as lived; and it is the form of the literary work that enables us, and indeed almost forces us, to make that connection. The passage at the end of the Nun's Priest's tale, by involving us in impenetrable ambiguity, calls attention to that paradox for the tale of Chauntecleer. But the passage also looks back to the other tale that is most clearly a "folye," to show that the notion of literature as pure entertainment, as pure distraction, is itself paradoxical. *Sir Thopas* is ultimately "drasty speche" not because it *is* worthless—no speech is worthless, according to the Nun's Priest's interpretation of St. Paul—but because it *would be* worthless if it were really what it pretends to be.

Prudence's argument in the *Melibeus* to justify apparent evil is the

103

standard Boethian argument that man's perception is partial. Her argument is also perfectly consistent with Christian doctrine. As such it is philosophically the most difficult argument to refute. The Nun's Priest's tale does not really refute the argument so much as it dismisses it as irrelevant for dealing in this world with the problem of evil. Much of the rhetorical elaboration of the Nun's Priest's tale is directly or indirectly concerned with this argument, but I would like to look most closely at lines 3232-55. The Nun's Priest apostrophizes the cock:

> Thou were ful wel ywarned by thy dremes
> That thilke day was perilous to thee;
> But what that God forwoot moot nedes bee,
> After the opinioun of certein clerkes.

And there follows a long discussion of the "greet disputisoun" over "symple necessitee" and "necessitee condicioneel," from which the Nun's Priest emerges none the wiser;

> I wol not han to do of swich mateere;
> My tale is of a cok, as ye may heere,
> That tok his conseil of his wyf, with sorwe. . . .

These last lines of course seem directly to contradict the passage about *moralite* at the end of the tale. It is typical of the attitude in the tale toward *moralite* that the Nun's Priest turns down a splendid opportunity for moralizing, and in the very next lines is moralizing again. The passage about simple and conditional necessity *sounds* thoroughly confusing, and would no doubt sound more so in oral delivery.[47] In any case the point made at the surface of the passage is that few people can understand the complex theological and philosophical arguments about foreknowledge and free will—and perhaps even the theologians and philosophers do not understand them. The arguments might just be so much tangled verbiage, like this passage of the Nun's Priest's tale.

I am more concerned, however, not with God's foreknowledge, but with human foreknowledge. In the tale, and in Chauntecleer's many exempla, God shares His foreknowledge with men through the agency of prophetic dreams. Genuinely prophetic dreams are possible, of course, only if there is a fixed Providential order of the universe. If all events are contingent, then human foreknowledge of those events must be contingent. In the *Melibeus*, Prudence on the allegorical level is the human faculty that projects the future. When we act with prudence, we act by projecting what will happen, given such-and-such conditions, and we choose the appropriate behavior accordingly. That is what "taking counsel" is all about. But where there are prophetic dreams, we already have knowledge of what will happen. The difficulty is only to determine whether the dream is genuinely prophetic. Prudence's way of dealing with the problem of evil is to argue that man's perception is partial—essentially, that he cannot judge conclusively that something is evil, because he does not know how things are going to turn out. But where we have prophetic dreams, we do know how things are going to turn out. And how does that affect our actions? We have, on the human level, a problem of foreknowledge and free will corresponding to the theological problem that the Nun's Priest refuses to deal with. Assuming that "dremes been to drede," that we have a genuinely prophetic dream, what should we do about it? If our foreknowledge is genuine, then no action we take will alter the outcome. On the other hand, if we take no action, then we are implicitly asserting that the dream has no purpose. And if the dream has no purpose, why has it become part of the Providential order of a reasonable (and presumably economical) God? Is human foreknowledge that results from prophetic dreams, in other words, a matter of "symple necessitee" or of "necessitee condicioneel"?

In all of Chauntecleer's examples of prophetic dreams, either the dream does the dreamer good because the appropriate action is taken; or the dream does no good because either the dreamer or someone else fails to take the appropriate action. In all of the exempla, then, dreams might seem to have a definite function—at least, so Chauntecleer asserts. They can warn men, and those who ignore them do so at their peril. Ironically, Chauntecleer himself becomes an exemplum of one whose prophetic dream does him no good because he ignores it, as the Nun's Priest emphasizes in the passage above. The point is this: as long as the dreams refer to "necessitee condicioneel," it is easy to see their function in the Providential order as warnings that can bring good out of evil. But if dreams refer to "symple necessitee," it is very hard to see what function they can have in the Providential order. God presumably has foreknowledge of how Chauntecleer is going to ignore his dream. What function, then, in the Providential economy does it serve to warn Chauntecleer of the bad thing that is going to happen to him? The theological answer that God gives perverse men these dreams to remove any excuse, to make clear that the responsibility for their folly and evil rests on them alone, very quickly leads us back into the very problem the tales of this fragment have up to now been trying to avoid—the problem of evil. For if the Providential order has determined all things, it has also determined that the perverse will be perverse. Are they free to perform good actions? And if so, in what sense? The problem of evil arises again in a new form, as the problem of foreknowledge versus free will.

More specifically, this passage in the Nun's Priest's tale calls into question the value of having knowledge about what is going to happen. Chauntecleer does not profit from his foreknowledge. The rhetorical stance adopted by Prudence in dealing with the problem of evil makes two assumptions: 1) man's knowledge is partial, and therefore we can "presume" or "conjecture" that apparent evil is really the Providence of a just and reasonable God; 2) it is important for man to attempt to repair his partial knowledge, even to project the future, by means of his rational faculty. The material on dreams, foreknowledge, and free will in the Nun's Priest's tale suggests that these two assumptions are incompatible. To the extent that we get foreknowledge, repair the partiality of our knowledge through prophetic dreams, the problem of evil does not diminish but becomes ever more acute. The warning dream that repairs man's partial knowledge is either useless—an impossibility in the Providential order of a just and reasonable God—or it thrusts before man the problem of evil in a form that cannot be gotten rid of merely by pleading ignorance.

The Nun's Priest's tale in lines 3204-13 seems specifically to mock the Monk's tale:

> But sodeynly hym fil a sorweful cas,
> For evere the latter ende of joye is wo.
> God woot that worldly joye is soone ago;
> And if a rethor koude faire endite,
> He in a cronycle saufly myghte it write
> As for a sovereyn notabilitee.
> Now every wys man, lat him herkne me;
> This storie is also trewe, I undertake,
> As is the book of Launcelot de Lake,
> That wommen holde in ful greet reverence.

The lines perhaps mock the Monk's pedantic definition of the term *tragedie*, by suggesting that his "tragedies" were in fact more like chronicles, mere reporting of events without concern for artistic arrangement. In any case, the passage suggests that one way to take the story of Chauntecleer is as a parody of the Monk's tragedies.[48] The joke in the first part of the passage, however, is that the "lesson" to be learned from the tragedies is a simple-minded one that everyday observation is sufficient to teach—"worldly joye is soone ago." From one point of view, the observation is certainly no "sovereyn notabilitee." It is something everybody knows already. The joke in the second part of the passage seems to be that precisely to the extent that literature is removed from what everybody knows already, it is "untrue." The ladies revere the book of Lancelot because the story is exotic. Thus, the passage points out a fundamental contradiction in the rhetorical stance of the Monk's tale. Rhetorical elevation in the tragedies aims at making the experiences of the protagonists something special, a spectacle far removed from the ordinary run of experience. And yet, in the "morals" of the tragedies, the simple-minded, philosophically trivial point is made again and again that worldly joy ends. So a rhetorical puffing-up devoted to demonstrating that Fortune is something special in particular cases ends up making the point that bad Fortune is general. The "lesson" is either inapplicable because we are not the mighty of the earth, or it is trivial. The mock-epic mode of the Nun's Priest's tale reinforces the point. When we see through the puffy rhetoric to the situation as it is, we see not a hero, but a rooster. When we see through the rhetoric of the Monk's tale, we see that after all the Boccaccian tragedies are just stories of men, and therefore have little to teach us.

The Nun's Priest's tale, then, uncovers paradoxes in the rhetorical stances of the other tales in the fragment. If these paradoxes were attributable just to intellectual deficiences of the tellers of these tales, then the Nun's Priest's tale would not be nearly so big an explosion as I think it is. But in fact these paradoxes are inherent in language itself, and so the Nun's Priest's tale becomes a profound indictment of the pretensions of school rhetoric in particular, and of literary art in general. Language itself is paradoxical, as we have come more and more to appreciate in this century—but of course, the philosophers of Chaucer's time and, I would argue, Chaucer himself knew that already.[49] The paradox in the Shipman's tale turns on our inability to decide whether language is merely secondary, a sign for a reality external to it, or whether it in some sense creates the reality it names—whether, to use a pair of terms fashionable in discussing Romantic poetry, language is mirror or lamp. Is the cultural, linguistic reality everything, or is there some brute, intractable reality external to and uncomprehended by language? The paradox in the Prioress' tale results from her inability to decide what meaning is—whether meaning is just the response of the hearer (in this case, pathos), or whether there is independent "objective" meaning that validates the individual response. Is the Prioress silly and sentimental, or is the human affective response profoundly in tune with reality? The paradox that underlies *Sir Thopas* is the old paradox of form versus content. Are linguistic utterances essentially form, essentially rule-governed (grammar, syntax, and ultimately genre); or are they essentially content, essentially free expression of individual, unique meanings? The paradox of the *Melibeus* is the paradox of inexpressible truth. In one sense, truth, as something that can be predicated of utterances, is immanent in language. We can know the truth, Prudence

107

argues, by taking counsel properly. In another sense, truth, as an attribute of God, is something that is impossible to comprehend in language. God's providence is ultimately inscrutable, says Prudence. We are unable to decide which view of language to take, and either one we take soon leads us into irreconcilable difficulties. Finally, the paradox underlying the Monk's tale is the paradox of interpretation itself, the paradox that has been named the "hermeneutic circle." We cannot understand the Monk's tale (or any work) unless we already know in general what it is about. We must already understand the lesson the tragedies teach, in an important sense, in order to understand the stories whose purpose is to teach that lesson.

My point is that these paradoxes are not functions of particular pilgrims or particular tales. They seem to be inherent in the fabric of language itself. They are precisely the kinds of problems that Wittgenstein called "deep"—they haunt us whenever we use language, because of the nature of the linguistic act; and we do not ever succeed in escaping from them by means of linguistic explanation. The existence of such paradoxes calls into question the validity of language itself as a mode of knowing and a mode of acting in the world.

Several critics have pointed out the affinities between the Nun's Priest's tale and *Troilus and Criseyde*.[50] Many of the same problems— such as dreams, predestination, foreknowledge, free will—that loom so large and are treated so seriously in *Troilus and Criseyde* receive a comic treatment in the Nun's Priest's tale. One could also compile a small anthology from criticism of the last decade or so in which the narrator of *Troilus and Criseyde*, in some aspects to be equated with the poet himself, is identified with Pandarus in that poem.[51] It is interesting to speculate that in the Nun's Priest's tale Chaucer is probing in a comic way the same painful subject dealt with seriously in *Troilus and Criseyde*—namely, the poet's responsibility for what he writes. Given that language is as paradoxical as the Nun's Priest shows it to be, can the poet himself ever be anything other than a Pandarus? The explicit moral the cock gives his experience is that one should avoid flattery. The moral the fox sees in it is that one should avoid "jangling." But *flaterye* and *janglynge*, flattery and idle talk, are precisely the means by which Pandarus gets his way in *Troilus and Criseyde*. Is the same sort of thing true of the poet? Is poetry all merely flattery (including man's self-flattery) or idle talk? If we cannot somehow deal with the paradoxes inherent in language itself, we can never know for sure.

And so the whole of *The Canterbury Tales* explodes in our faces, precisely to the extent that we accept this most seductive world-view of the Nun's Priest's tale.[52] Thus, the consideration of the problem of evil is temporarily suspended to deal with a more immediate problem for author and reader—the problem of language. Until that problem is somehow dealt with, it is mere presumption to attempt to talk away the problem of evil. And this, finally, is the *moralite* of the Nun's Priest's tale.

CHAPTER EIGHT

Fragments VIII-IX:
The Problem of Language, Continued

The explosion in the Nun's Priest's tale raises the spectre of the uncreative Word, the antithesis of the ordering Word of the gospel of John. The poet and the reader become anti-creators, makers of the illusory, perverse worlds of mere rhetoric. The tale asks whether we can trust language. If we cannot, how can we know anything at all? Language, the creative Word, is the means of transmitting the knowledge necessary for salvation. If language fails, if in fact all man's linguistic efforts are structures floating unsupported in the air, then we are left with a very dark view indeed of the value of consciousness and of the possibilities for redemption of human experience. The tales that follow the Nun's Priest's tale explore the limits of language, either in an attempt to ground language in something transcendently true, or in an attempt to show what language can never be called upon to perform. The Second Nun's tale is optimistic about language, showing how linguistically transmitted knowledge can be grounded in visionary experience. The Canon's Yeoman's tale is pessimistic, arguing that language cannot be grounded in material reality, that there is no such thing as the "scientific" or purely referential use of language where words can be set in one-to-one correspondence with material objects. The Manciple is pessimistic for a different reason. His tale demonstrates the impossibility of grounding language in culture, in man's understanding of the human world he inhabits. It is interesting that in the Manciple's prologue, as in his tale, telling the truth in unequivocal speech brings about a breakdown in the social order. When the Manciple describes the drunken Cook, no doubt quite accurately, the Cook grows angry and the Manciple is threatened with exposure of his dishonest "rekenynges" (74). And the breach is repaired not by means of language —indeed, the Cook is actually too drunk to speak—but by a gift of wine, an exchange of substance. The Manciple's tale then explores the futility of dealing linguistically with the human world—its moral is "Kepe wel thy tonge" (362).

I see the Manciple's tale as a kind of contrast to the Canon's Yeoman's tale. And several critics have seen the Second Nun's tale and Canon's Yeoman's tale as a contrasting pair, where Cecilia is concerned with spiritual vision and spiritual work, and the Canon's Yeoman is concerned with empirical knowledge and the theologically suspect alchemical "work." I shall concentrate on the views of language in the tales, to show how they fit into the structure I am describing. But of course, they contrast with each other on many different levels.[1]

The Second Nun's Tale

Trevor Whittock says that in this tale poetic techniques "transform the nature of language: words and phrases acquire a mystical significance over and above their literal denotation."[2] Language, then, is valuable. It is not mere rhetoric, precisely because *in itself* it is nothing. It is valuable because it points beyond itself to the truth in which it is grounded.[3]

The theme of "work" that is so important in the Second Nun's tale is closely related to the question of the validity of language. Most of Cecilia's "work" consists in teaching or in preaching (152 ff., 284 ff., 342, 414, 538-39). But "works" are traditionally, as in line 64 of the prologue, opposed to "faith": "feith is deed withouten werkis." Faith implies, among other things, belief in certain propositional truths, and it is extremely important in the tale for the converted to assent to these truths. Valerian cannot see the angel unless he agrees to "trowe on Crist" and be baptized (171). Tiburce sees the angel only after Pope Urban has "made hym in that place / Parfit in his lernynge" (352-53). And the people are converted when they give "ful credence / Unto hire word" (415-16). But the belief, the assenting to propositional truth, is validated not by linguistic argument, but by deeds. Cecilia's apparent obnoxiousness in confronting Almachius comes partly from her realization that argument is vain.[4] Argument alone will not persuade the perverse. Cecilia thus merely rebukes Almachius' stupidity. The tale as a whole shows what Cecilia implicitly recognizes, namely that language must be grounded in some deeper level of truth from which it takes its value.

Cecilia, Valerian, Tiburce, and Maximus all achieve direct access to that deeper level of truth in visions, and that access is what makes them capable of converting others through linguistic means:

> This Maximus, that saugh this thyng bityde,
> With pitous teeris tolde it anonright,
> That he hir soules saugh to hevene glyde

111

> With aungels ful of cleernesse and of light,
> And with his word converted many a wight.   (400-04)

Valerian asks for a vision as proof of Cecilia's preaching (163-64). After he seeks out Urban, he is himself granted a vision that grounds his belief in the propositional truth of the articles of the Creed. An "oold man" (201), presumably St. Paul, appears to Valerian, and he has "a book with lettre of gold in honde" (202), from which he reads, asking,

> "Leevestow this thyng or no? Sey ye or nay."
> "I leeve al this thyng," quod Valerian,
> "For sother thyng than this, I dar wel say,
> Under the hevene no wight thynke may."   (212-15)

It is interesting that the old man reads the book (or so I take it, though there is perhaps some ambiguity), suggesting that the propositions of the faith are grounded in the validity of the vision, and not the other way around. Belief in linguistic expression of spiritual truths comes through vision, and is a special power granted to the saved and withheld from the perverse.

The case of Tiburce is similar. The first step in his conversion is his smelling of the crowns that he is unable yet to see (251-52)—he is actually changed by the olfactory revelation, redeemed so that he is capable of hearing and receiving the instruction from Cecilia and Pope Urban that will make him "Parfit in his lernynge" (353):

> Valerian seyde: "Two corones han we,
> Snow white and rose reed, that shynen cleere,
> Whiche that thyne eyen han no myght to see;
> And as thou smellest hem thurgh my preyere,
> So shaltow seen hem, leeve brother deere,
> If it so be thou wolt, withouten slouthe,
> Bileve aright and knowen verray trouthe."   (253-59)

All the conversions in the tale, then, come through preaching and instruction, but they rest directly or indirectly on the validity of visions.

In her dialogue with Almachius, Cecilia makes two important points about language. First, she rebukes Almachius several times for speaking falsely and foolishly (450-51, 466-67, 479, 485-86). Cecilia is not just attempting to hasten her martyrdom. The suggestion is that there is some ultimate standard in terms of which to judge truth at every level of discourse, and that those who fail to judge by this standard make fools of themselves in debate. The power of argument, in other words, of logic and dialectic, depends for its validity on the perception of spiritual reality, just as the power of creedal statement does. Language is not an

112

independent construction that pulls itself up by its own bootstraps, as it were, and works by its own rules. It is instead a part of the creation that draws its power from the Creator who sustains it. To lose sight of the fact is to become a fool even in terms of the internal rules of the language-game. Cecilia's other point is that language is not independent of the material world, either:

> Ther lakketh no thyng to thyne outter yen
> That thou n'art blynd; for thyng that we seen alle
> That it is stoon,—that men may wel espyen,—
> That ilke stoon a god thow wolt it calle.
> I rede thee, lat thyn hand upon it falle,
> And taste it wel, and stoon thou shalt it fynde,
> Syn that thou seest nat with thyne eyen blynde.   (498-504)

Cecilia suggests that our bodily senses do not deceive us, but that error is a matter of spiritual blindness. Furthermore, language does bear some definite relation to material reality. It is ultimately *wrong to call* the stone a god, and ultimately right to call it what our senses tell us it is, a stone. The Canon's Yeoman's tale will take up in more detail this question of the relation between language and material objects. But in the world-view of the Second Nun's tale the relation is quite simple. Material objects are what they seem, because God does not deceive us through our senses. And we know the proper names for them, as we know the propositional truth of the articles of Christian faith, because everything in human experience is grounded in divine reality.

The Second Nun's tale thus proposes a solution for the linguistic difficulties raised by the Nun's Priest's tale. Language is valid, and the knowledge we get through language—knowledge both of the material world and of heaven—is valid to the extent that it is grounded in spiritual vision. But, as always, there is a problem. As Donald R. Howard observes, "The Second Nun's legend puts before us an ideal so high that all other ideals of civil, domestic, and private conduct vanish before it."[5] The ideal is indeed high, and impossible for most of us to attain, precisely because most of us do not have visions. The Second Nun's tale presents a view of language and experience that is theologically valid, in fourteenth-century terms, and philosophically consistent. But it is not really very helpful.[6]

The Canon's Yeoman's Tale

Recent criticism of the Canon's Yeoman's tale takes its cue from Charles Muscatine's illuminating reading, which argues that the tale is about "alchemy as a blind materialism."[7] Thorough and persuasive articles by

Joseph E. Grennen[8] and Bruce A. Rosenburg[9] treat the Second Nun's tale and the Canon's Yeoman's tale as a contrasting pair, stressing mainly the oppositions between the unity of Cecilia's vision and the chaotic diversity of the alchemical "multiplying," between the spiritual "werk" of Cecilia and the materialistic alchemical "werk," and between the spiritual insight of the Second Nun's tale and the blindness of the alchemists. The Yeoman's apostrophe to alchemists is reminiscent of Cecilia's remarks to Almachius, when she accuses him of blindness because he worships a stone. The Yeoman says,

> Ye been as boold as is Bayard the blynde,
> That blondreth forth, and peril casteth noon.
> He is as boold to renne agayn a stoon
> As for to goon bisides in the weye. (1413-16)

The stone the alchemists "run against" in their blindness is the philosopher's stone, which usurps the place of God in their lives as the idol usurps the place of God in Almachius' life; and the alchemists are thus turned aside from the true "weye" of salvation.[10]

The Canon's Yeoman's tale strikes deep chords in twentieth-century readers, because of our oppressive concern about the abuse of technology. But I want to concentrate on what the tale shows about the limitations of language. What it shows is obvious: language cannot cope with the material world considered in and of itself. In the Second Nun's tale, Cecilia can know that a stone is just a stone, because she perceives the material world in the proper context of spiritual reality. In the Canon's Yeoman's tale, the alchemist cannot know what a stone is, because he attempts to understand matter in itself, divorced from the spiritual reality that sustains it and makes it intelligible.

The attempt to deal with matter linguistically takes two different forms in the Canon's Yeoman's tale. The first is the enormous proliferation of technical terminology evident in the Yeoman's description of the alchemists' chemicals, tools, and processes (lines 750-861). The use of language here is a methodological nominalism—technical terms are invented and the vocabulary grows and grows so that the "scientist" may approximate more and more closely to the "ideal" condition in which each object has its unique, arbitrarily assigned name. Of course, in the process the possibility of generalizing, and therefore of having scientific knowledge, disappears. "Lo! which avantage is to multiplie! / That slidynge science hath me maad so bare" (731-32). The multiplying is also of course multiplying of terms, and the Yeoman seems explicitly to recognize that, in a pun at the end of the tale: "certes, never shal he thryve, / Thogh that he multiplie terme of his lyve" (1478-79). The "science" of alchemy is "slidynge" partly, at least, because the more one seems to know (that is, the more things he has names for), the less he actually knows, because the diversity of his multiplying terms has stripped him of generalizing power. The Yeoman specifically mentions the technical terminology several times, suggesting that the only real good of the terms is to conceal the alchemists' ignorance: "we semen wonder wise, / Oure termes been so clergial and so queynte" (751-52); "For in his termes he wol hym so wynde, / And speke his wordes in so sly a kynde" (980-81); "They mowe wel chiteren as doon thise jayes, / And in hir termes sette hir lust and peyne" (1397-98).

Though he emphasizes the piling-up of technical terms, the Canon's Yeoman emphasizes perhaps even more the vanity of the alchemists' enterprise. The alchemists fail again and again, at everything except gulling innocents. One point of the Yeoman's tale is that the validity of language cannot be made to depend upon the material world. Language cannot derive its being as a kind of secondary being, dependent on the things it names, for we do not understand the being of the material objects themselves apart from language. And if, by methodological nominalism, we begin to sever the word from the thing—that is, to admit the arbitrariness of the connection between word and thing— both language and matter become unintelligible. Perhaps both matter and language, and their relation, can be rendered intelligible through a vision of spiritual reality, as in the tale of St. Cecilia. But that is still cold comfort for those of us who do not have visions. We are left with the linguistic world and the world of matter, and apparently it does not work to ground language in matter. If there is no inherently valid connection between the word and the thing it names on the level of brute matter, the same might well be true on the level of any other kind of being we attempt to understand and control by means of language.

Thus, we come to the second form of the attempt in the Canon's Yeoman's tale to deal with matter linguistically. In lines 1428 ff., the Yeoman, following the lead of the alchemical treatises he cites, talks about chemicals and chemical processes in an apparently *allegorical* mode:

> He seith how that the dragon, doutelees,
> Ne dyeth nat, but if that he be slayn
> With his brother; and that is for to sayn,
> By the dragon, Mercurie,

and so on. But the conclusion of Arnold of the New Town, and apparently of the Canon's Yeoman, is as follows:

Lat no man bisye hym this art for to seche,
But if that he th'entencioun and speche
Of philosophres understonde kan.   (1442-44)

In other words, one must already understand the speech of alchemists—
the allegory, that is—for the allegory to make sense. The allegory is not a
means of instruction, not a means of conveying knowledge, for it is
meaningless to the man who does not already understand it. And
anyone who approaches the allegory in any other spirit is a "lewed
man" (1445). One does not gain knowledge, but only demonstrates his
folly.

Plato's student, similarly, asks for verbal instruction about the philosopher's stone, and Plato replies by presenting a series of apparently
meaningless names: "Titanos" (1454), "Magnasia" (1455), "water that
is maad, I seye, / Of elementes foure" (1459-60). As the pupil responds,
"This is *ignotum per ignocius*" (1457). Language becomes an infinite chain
of significations that never terminates in a material object that can be
known. The answer the pupil seeks, as Plato says, is the secret of the
philosophers, and they have sworn not to reveal it,

For unto Crist it is so lief and deere
That he wol not that it discovered bee,
But where it liketh to his deitee
Men for t'enspire.   (1467-70)

The possibility of this knowledge rests on special inspiration. It is not
revealed through human language. The essence of understanding allegory, of course, is that one must somehow be capable of penetrating the
husk and laying bare the kernel. There is no scientific procedure, no set
of verbal instructions, that makes one capable of performing this
mysterious fundamental act of interpretation. Ultimately, the allegorical mode of dealing with matter depends on prior spiritual insight into
the matter itself and into the connection between the matter and the
language used to talk about it.

And so, in a sense, we have made no progress since the Second Nun's
tale. Knowledge and the valid use of language still seem to depend on
vision, on special inspiration that most of us lack most or all of the time.
The Canon's Yeoman's tale explores a dead end—the futility of the
alchemists' endeavor is in part the futility of attempting to ground
language in matter. Matter is not to be the firm, intelligible foundation
it seems, and thus it is not the proper terminus of human inquiry. Once
we abstract from the possibility of the rare visionary visitation, the
question of the validity of language for dealing with ordinary human
experience—a question of ultimate importance for the poet—is left
hanging.

Most critics recognize that language is a crucial issue in the Manciple's tale.[11] I think the tale forms a pair with the Canon's Yeoman's tale: the Manciple's tale explores the futility of attempting to ground language in culturally determined reality, just as the Canon's Yeoman's tale explores the futility of attempting to ground it in matter.

The Manciple's tale makes its point in several ways. First, there is the "digression" (207-37) concerning the relationship between "word" and "werkyng." The Manciple argues here, essentially, that a culture, by tacit agreement (convention) may erect a distinction where there is none, strictly by verbal means: "She shal be *cleped* his lady," "She shal be *cleped* his wenche," "therfore is he *cleped* a capitayn," "Men *clepen* hym an outlawe or a theef." Language grounded in cultural agreement, then, obscures moral truth. And yet, the truth that is obscured is not a truth about the world of matter, merely. It is a truth about human relationships, a cultural truth. And in the realm of culture, there is in fact a difference between the lady and the wench, between the captain and the outlaw, precisely because the culture has determined that it shall be so. What is the reality, then? The Manciple's digression *says* that there is a reality prior to the cultural conventions of language, a "werkyng" that the word should correspond to if cultural conventions are to be rightly understood. But the tale *shows* rather that conventions are unintelligible. It is impossible to explain why one woman in the culture should be treated as a wench, and another as a lady; or why one man should be treated as a hero and another as a thief—and yet it is so. The point that the Manciple's digression makes is that cultural conventions are as unintelligible as matter is to the alchemists. To say that money and power explain the different uses of language accomplishes nothing, for money and power are themselves just cultural conventions. In the Canon's Yeoman's tale, we see that grounding language in matter, by assigning words as arbitrary counters for things, cannot work. Here we see that it will not work to ground language in culture by assigning words to things in accordance with conventional agreement. Making such assignments only points up acutely the unintelligibility of the conventions themselves. Language as convention shares the irrationality of all cultural convention.

The crow's experience makes a second point about the attempt to ground language in culture. A culture represents the common ground among its members, and so any cultural manifestation is bound to be more or less inadequate to unique individual experience. The crow's words, while they are historically true, fail because they are not adequate

117

to the experience of the individual human heart. Blunt historical truth fails to take into account the intensity of Phoebus' love and his capacity for self-deception. In his speech after he has killed his wife, as Britton J. Harwood points out,[12] Phoebus recreates his wife in a different image, essentially by describing her in a series of lies that correspond more closely to his experience of her than the crow's truth does. The speech is consciously rhetorical, and the tale seems to be making fun of Phoebus for allowing himself to be deceived by his own language. The irony here is double-edged, however. The truth does not suffice, because it must be articulated in conventional terms that can never satisfy the unique experience of the individual heart. On the other hand, lies are made possible by the same conventions of language that allow us to subsume individual experience under rhetorical modes that are inappropriate. Phoebus misjudges in one sense: he subsumes his case under the rhetoric of the loving husband who has slain a guiltless wife. In another sense, he does not misjudge, because that rhetoric is nearer to his experience than the crow's "Cokkow! cokkow! cokkow!" The paradox is inherent in language considered as convention. Historical truth misses the point of individual experience, but what is most adequate to individual experience is often not true. Truth itself becomes a matter of convention.

All that remains is silence, as the Manciple's tale reminds us again and again in lines 309-62. Repeating the moral for so many lines does more than to parody the genre of moral fable, I think. The point is that the advice is self-contradictory. If the best thing to do is to hold one's tongue, then the whole genre of the proverb or maxim is suspect. If Solomon had taken his own advice seriously, there would be no proverbs from him. And Chaucer makes the point perfectly clear by having the Manciple go much beyond what is necessary in a speech whose point is that one should not speak much. Here, as in the lines at the end of his "digression" (235-36), the Manciple says that he is "noght textueel" (316). And again, the point seems to be the futility of grounding language in cultural convention. We are again faced with paradox. Conventional wisdom bids us keep silent, but that wisdom itself must be embodied in linguistic utterance. Language, considered as social convention, cancels itself out precisely when we reach the point of recognizing it as convention, recognizing that it has no further explanation or justification. The effect of language is destructive of understanding, as it was (though in a different way) in the Canon's Yeoman's tale. "A tonge kutteth freendshipe al a-two" (342), destroying the mutual understanding that gives rise to language in the first place. The more we attempt to ground language in culture, the more we come face to face with the unintelligibility of cultural convention itself.

The last part of the Manciple's tale is thus not just a descent into the argument from expediency. A proverb is an attempt to articulate the conventional wisdom of a culture, something the culture has agreed to accept as "true." But the attempt is self-contradictory—to take the advice implies the impossibility of giving it. This situation exactly mirrors the logical paradox inherent in regarding language as cultural convention. The decision to regard language that way comes from a desire to validate language, to relate it to something outside itself which is "true" and against which linguistic utterance can be tested. But the essence of cultural convention is that it is not fixed or "true" apart from language, is not outside language. If language is convention, it both is and is not "true." And so the human world in the Manciple's tale becomes as unintelligible as the natural world is for the alchemists. As Donald R. Howard points out, the Manciple's "last words, if taken seriously, would nullify all authors and all 'tidings,' would nullify speech and story and literature."[13]

CHAPTER NINE

Fragment X:
Conclusion

In fragment X, we reach the end of the pilgrimage as we have it. *The Canterbury Tales* moves from fiction to non-fiction,[1] from the works to the Parson's tale which regards those works in terms of the orthodox ultimate categories, and finally to the poet himself. The setting sun and the "thropes ende" at the beginning of the Parson's prologue seem to dramatize the unintelligibility of the natural world and the human world, the theme built up in the preceding two tales.[2] The Parson rejects much of what we should call "literature,"[3] in favor of "Moralitee and vertuous mateere," necessary to "shewe yow the wey, in this viage, / Of thilke parfit glorious pilgrymage." He leaves the world of the pilgrimage, suddenly become dark and unintelligible, behind.[4]

The Parson's Tale

Most of what I would say about the Parson's tale has been said already. Others have pointed out its relations with the Knight's tale, as the spiritual pole toward which the pilgrimage, beginning with a secular vision, tends.[5] Others have mentioned its deep differences from the rest of the tales of the fictive pilgrimage.[6] But the strongest difference, at least between this tale and the immediately preceding tales, is that the Parson's tale redeems language. What it says it says obviously, didactically. What it shows, too, is obvious—its many resonances with the other tales and other pilgrims show that its system of ultimate categories is comprehensive. The all-encompassing category for the understanding of human experience, in the world-view of the Parson's tale, is sin. All experience, both that of the fictive world and that of the real world past, present, and future, can be understood adequately in terms of that category and its sub-categories. The understanding comes through verbal instruction, as in the Parson's tale itself. The validity of instruction rests on revelation—as interpreted in the orthodoxy of medieval Catholicism. The tale begins with a verse from Scripture and constantly quotes Scripture and the Fathers in support of the Parson's exhortations. Language is valid not because human beings can ground it in matter or in social convention, but because God has given and guaranteed His Word.

But the Word is sufficient only for that understanding which is necessary to man's salvation, and that is precisely an understanding of one's own sin and of how to deal with it. The pretensions of alchemical "science" to know the world, or of philosophy to know humanity, or of theology to know God, vanish in the recognition of man's limitation by sin. Language cannot help us know all of those things the Nun's Priest laughed at us for pretending to know. But language can help us know our own sin, and we must acknowledge sin to be saved. As the Parson translates his text, "Stondeth upon the weyes, and seeth and axeth of olde pathes (that is to seyn, of olde sentences) which is the goode wey, / and walketh in that wey, and ye shal fynde refresshynge for your soules" (77-78). Human beings are capable of judging "ways" (and language) to see which are good and which are bad, and we have the power because God has given it to us: "Oure sweete Lord God of hevene, that no man wole perisse, but wole that we comen alle to the knoweleche of hym, and to the blisful lif that is perdurable, / amonesteth us by the prophete Jeremie" (75-76). The Parson's tale is not so much a sermon as it is a penitential manual, a treatise "of instruction for the priest dealing specifically with the sacrament of penance."[7] The tale is an answer, then, indeed *the* orthodox answer, to the deep questionings of the validity of language that have gone on in the last part of *The Canterbury Tales*. The point is not so much that the Parson alludes to all the pilgrims and their tales. The point is rather that the Parson's tale, more than any other, provides us with a system of categories to understand all human experience. And the validity of what it has to say rests ultimately on divine relevation.

If the vision of the Parson's tale is complete—at least from the perspective of fourteenth-century Catholicism—that does not mean that it is completely satisfying. Whittock argues that even in this tale we find Chaucer's own "multidimensional ambiguity."[8] Chaucer's tactic is to explore many paths, and the Parson's is just one path. The Parson is not Chaucer. But the last tale in *The Canterbury Tales* leaves me not with a sense that Chaucer is pointing out the Parson's limitations or the limitations of orthodoxy, but instead with a sense that Chaucer is accepting his own limitations. Accepting one's own limitations is necessary for salvation, whether secular or spiritual; but it is never satisfying. That is only to say that life is imperfect and that we are imperfect, that we are fallen. But that very dissatisfaction, that awareness of sin, is precisely the religious impulse which stirs us up to seek God. Thus, the form of *The Canterbury Tales* is validated in the moment of its rejection. What we learn from the work is to be dissatisfied with this life, and what we learn from that dissatisfaction is to turn to God.

The Retractation

The Retractation follows naturally, then, almost inevitably, from everything that has gone before. It is "genuine" in my reading of *The
Canterbury Tales*, because in my reading it makes no sense to see Chaucer
as a fore-runner of the Renaissance, an author rising on the wings of
language to celebrate the greatness of humanity. Instead, *The Canterbury
Tales* accepts man's sinfulness, his limitations as a fallen creature, and
accepts too the distortions and limitations of his language.[9] Whether or
not the historical Chaucer speaks here, the Retractation is so presented,
and in my reading that presentation is "right." Speaking historically,
judging the historical Chaucer's mind from his work, I think it likely
that the historical Chaucer would have questioned his own ability to
know his mind well enough to make such retractions and make them
sincerely. The Parson's tale assures us that we can know and reject our
own sin, but nowhere does it assure us that the enterprise is easy.

For the historical Chaucer, the tales in the collection must have
appeared in some sense much as this reading has taken them—that is, as
embodiments of certain world-views to be seriously entertained and
then accepted or rejected. All of the tales that are not direct translations
or adaptations presumably had close analogues with which Chaucer
was familiar. Their world-views, then, were not his invention, but
something he transmitted to his audience. The closing description in the
Ellesmere manuscript of Chaucer as the one who "compiled" *The
Canterbury Tales*,[10] whether it is Chaucerian or not, has a certain
aptness. The structure I have proposed is to a degree open-ended.
Chaucer could have finished the Cook's tale, or even the Squire's tale.
Within limits, he could have added other tales of certain types to certain
existing groups. Presumably the over-arching view of the world that
emerges is Chaucer's own, or close to it. It need not be so. The author
who wears so many masks in the course of *The Canterbury Tales* and his
other works is surely capable of sustaining another one. But reading *The
Canterbury Tales* as I have read it does produce a definite structure that
might allow us to use the work as evidence for inferring how the
historical Chaucer might have looked at the world. And that reading is
consistent with the assumption that the Retractation is genuine insofar
as any such human statement can be genuine—a possibility called into
question by the work itself. Ultimately, then, the value of *The Canterbury
Tales* is to make us question the enterprise it involves us in—the
enterprise of literature itself, involving author, reader, and now critic.
The hope it holds forth is the hope of Christian orthodoxy—the hope of
salvation. The lesson it teaches is the lesson of humility.

NOTES

[1] "Tales of the Homeward Journey," *Studies in Philology*, 28 (1931), 85 [617].

[2] "The Alternative Reading of *The Canterbury Tales*: Chaucer's Text and the Early Manuscripts," *PMLA*, 97 (1982), 246-47. Larry D. Benson, "The Order of *The Canterbury Tales*," *Studies in the Age of Chaucer*, 3 (1981), 77-120, has reassessed the manuscript evidence, concluding that the Ellesmere order "represents Chaucer's own final arrangement" (p. 79). But Benson's argument depends on his reading of the Retractation, which (as Benson believes) indicates Chaucer's intention to stop working on his unfinished work: "We have, in short, . . . Chaucer's final version, as it was when he decided his work on it was ended" (p. 80). The theoretical point here is this: even if we accept Benson's argument about the *order* of the tales, we still are not justified in drawing interpretive conclusions from that order about the *structure* of the whole work. Manly's and Owen's point still holds. If Chaucer thought of the work as unfinished—which Benson admits—then it would be unintelligible to talk about a "definite plan" on Chaucer's part as reflected in the manuscripts. There are two possibilities: either Chaucer had no definite plan for the finished work (his "plan" was developing as he went along); or else Chaucer had a definite plan for the finished work which he did not carry out. We cannot infer that definite plan, however, from the provisional tale-order of the unfinished work, even if we agree that that order is Chaucer's own. The Ellesmere order reflects *a* structure, certainly, but not *the* structure of *The Canterbury Tales*. Helen Cooper, *The Structure of the Canterbury Tales* (Athens: University of Georgia Press, 1984), p. 61, also makes this point. See also N. F. Blake, "Critics, Criticism and the Order of *The Canterbury Tales*," *Archiv für das Studium der Neueren Sprachen und Literaturen*, 218 (1) (1981), 47-58.

[3] And there is of course some doubt that there is consensus. Though modern editors (notably F. N. Robinson and John H. Fisher) adopt the Ellesmere order, as recently as 1978 George R. Keiser wrote "In Defense of the Bradshaw Shift," *Chaucer Review*, 12, 191-201. And a more recent editor, Norman Blake, *The Canterbury Tales by Geoffrey Chaucer* (London: Edward Arnold, 1980), adopts the order of the Hengwrt manuscript—his base manuscript—with an elaborate explanation of how that order might have come about ("Introduction," pp. 6-10). Blake, however, describes the Hengwrt order as "a scribal one in so far as the arrangement of the sections is concerned, since Chaucer had not determined a final order by the time he died" (10).

[4] See, for example, Manly, "Tales of the Homeward Journey"; J. S. P. Tatlock, "*The Canterbury Tales* in 1400," *PMLA*, 50 (1935), 100-39; Germaine Dempster, "The Fifteenth Century Editors of the *Canterbury Tales* and the Problem of Tale-Order," *PMLA*, 64 (1949), 1123-42; Charles A. Owen,

Jr., "The Plan of the Canterbury Pilgrimage," *PMLA*, 66 (1951), 820-26, and "The Transformation of a Frame Story: The Dynamics of Fiction," in Rossell Hope Robbins, ed., *Chaucer at Albany* (New York: Franklin, 1975), pp. 125-46; and Edward S. Cohen, "The Sequence of the *Canterbury Tales*," *Chaucer Review*, 9 (1974), 190-95.

5 Lee S. Cox makes this point in "A Question of Order in the *Canterbury Tales*," *Chaucer Review*, 1 (1966-67), arguing that "no projected journey pattern is absolutely satisfactory" (237).

6 Germaine Dempster, "A Period in the Development of the Canterbury Tales Marriage Group and of Blocks B² and C," *PMLA*, 68 (1953), 1142-59.

7 Cox, "A Question of Order in the *Canterbury Tales*," pp. 239-52.

8 Richard L. Hoffman, "Jephthah's Daughter and Chaucer's Virginia," *Chaucer Review*, 2 (1967), 20-31; and Peter G. Beidler, "The Pairing of the *Franklin's Tale* and the *Physician's Tale*," *Chaucer Review*, 3 (1969), 275-79.

9 Various critics from Kittredge's day to the present have attacked the usual interpretation of the Marriage Group as being either fundamentally mistaken or as distracting from other themes treated in the tales of fragments III-V. Such critics are, among others, H. B. Hinckley, "The Debate on Marriage in the *Canterbury Tales*," *PMLA*, 32 (1917), 292-305; Clifford P. Lyons, "The Marriage Debate in the *Canterbury Tales*," *ELH*, 2 (1935), 252-62; Kemp Malone, "*The Wife of Bath's Tale*," *Modern Language Review*, 57 (1962), 481-91; W. G. East, "By Preeve Which That is Demonstratif," *Chaucer Review*, 12 (1977), 78-82; and Judson Boyce Allen and Theresa Anne Moritz, *A Distinction of Stories: The Medieval Unity of Chaucer's Fair Chain of Narratives for Canterbury* (Columbus: Ohio State University Press, 1981), who thoroughly reorder the tales of the Marriage Group (see especially pp. 106-07). See also Cooper, *The Structure of the Canterbury Tales*, p. 125.

NOTES TO CHAPTER TWO

1 *Of Sondry Folk: The Dramatic Principle in The Canterbury Tales* (Austin: University of Texas Press, 1955).

2 Athens: University of Georgia Press, 1984. The quotations are from p. 69. Another recent thematic reading is that of Traugott Lawler, *The One and the Many in the Canterbury Tales* (Hamden, Connecticut: Archon Books, 1980), who sees the "complementary relationship" between "oneness and multiplicity" as "the most pervasive issue in the poem, and its major unifying force." Not everyone in Kittredge's day read *The Canterbury Tales* dramatically, of course. A good counter-example is Frederick Tupper, "Chaucer and the Seven Deadly Sins," *PMLA*, 29 (1914), 93-128, who sees Chaucer's tales as exempla told against each of the Deadly Sins. Nor does everyone nowadays read the tales thematically. A good example of a recent book that still takes the dramatic approach to a large extent is Charles A. Owen, Jr., *Pilgrimage and Storytelling in the Canterbury Tales: The Dialectic of "Ernest" and "Game"* (Norman: University of Oklahoma Press, c1977). Owen says that in *The Canterbury Tales* "The game of storytelling replaces the 'ernest' of overt morality as the source of value" (p. 3).

3 In G. L. Kittredge, *Chaucer and His Poetry* (Cambridge: Harvard University Press, 1915), pp. 154 ff.

[4] I think especially of R. E. Kaske's discussion "Chaucer's Marriage Group," in *Chaucer the Love Poet*, ed. Jerome Mitchell and William Provost (Athens: University of Georgia Press, c1973), pp. 43-65.

[5] William Witherle Lawrence, for example, in *Chaucer and the Canterbury Tales* (New York: Columbia University Press, 1950), adopts the Bradshaw shift and maintains that the Marriage Group begins with the Tale of Melibeus and includes also the Nun's Priest's tale.

[6] Kittredge, pp. 154-55.

[7] *The Unity of the Canterbury Tales*, *Anglistica* 5 (Copenhagen: Rosenkilde and Bagger, 1955).

[8] *A Preface to Chaucer: Studies in Medieval Perspectives* (Princeton, N. J.: Princeton University Press, 1963).

[9] *A Reading of the Canterbury Tales* (Albany: State University of New York Press, 1964).

[10] The best discussion and confrontation of opposing viewpoints that I know of is still the little volume edited by Dorothy Bethurum, *Critical Approaches to Medieval Literature: Selected Papers from the English Institute, 1958-59* (New York: Columbia University Press, 1960). This volume contains splendid essays by E. Talbot Donaldson (for the opposition) and R. E. Kaske (for the defense). For a discussion of the theoretical issues involved in historical criticism, see my article "The Raven and the Writing Desk: The Theoretical Limits of Patristic Criticism," *Chaucer Review*, 14 (1980), 260-77.

[11] *Chaucer and the Shape of Creation: The Aesthetic Possibilities of Inorganic Structure* (Cambridge: Harvard University Press, 1967).

[12] *A Reading of the Canterbury Tales* (London: Cambridge University Press, 1968).

[13] See, for example, Norman E. Eliason, *The Language of Chaucer's Poetry*, *Anglistica* 17 (Copenhagen: Rosenkilde and Bagger, 1972), pp. 140, 180; and William Frost, "What Is A Canterbury Tale?" in *Western Humanities Review*, 27 (1973), 39-59. Cooper, *The Structure of the Canterbury Tales*, approaches the work in the light of other medieval story-collections, where "story-collection" is conceived as a generic category.

[14] Berkeley: The University of California Press, c1976. The quotation is from p. 1.

[15] Allen and Moritz, *A Distinction of Stories*, use the classifications of Ovid's tales, developed by medieval commentators, to classify Chaucer's tales, gathering the tales into four types and proposing a new ordering that is not based on the manuscripts or on geography. They justify their ordering by arguing that it is "heuristically correct. It works. It grounds our reading" (p. 98). I find two difficulties with Allen and Moritz's procedure. First, some might find them entirely too cavalier about manuscript evidence. Even if manuscript evidence is to be pushed to the horizon in an inquiry about the structure of *The Canterbury Tales*, nevertheless the evidence remains on the horizon as a limit to what it is possible to say. The second difficulty is their argument that using medieval commentaries on Ovid renders their reading "medieval." In the model of interpretation they adopt, one where the justification of a model is only that "it works," to show that the resulting reading is "medieval" is jejune. The commentaries on Ovid merely provide a critical vocabulary for articulating one's understanding—one vocabulary of many possible ones,

125

medieval and modern. The use of these medieval commentaries does not give Allen and Moritz's interpretation any special historical status.

16 *Speculum*, 52 (1977), 997.

17 *PMLA*, 69 (1954), 928-36; rpt. in E. T. Donaldson, *Speaking of Chaucer*, (London: Athlone Press, University of London, c1970), pp. 1-12.

18 "The Personality of Chaucer the Pilgrim," *PMLA*, 75 (1960), 160.

19 "The Art of Impersonation: A General Prologue to the *Canterbury Tales*," *PMLA*, 95 (1980), 215.

20 I mean here something on a more fundamental level than the dramatic interactions on the pilgrimage that seem to comment on poetry—such as the Knight's stinting of the Monk, the Franklin's stinting (perhaps) of the Squire, the Parson's comment on alliterative poetry, or even the subtle mockery of Harry Bailly as a literary critic that Alan Gaylord finds in fragment VII—see "*Sentence* and *Solaas* in Fragment VII of the *Canterbury Tales*: Harry Bailly as Horseback Editor," *PMLA*, 82 (1967), 226-35.

21 In *The Strumpet Muse: Art and Morals in Chaucer's Poetry* (Bloomington: Indiana University Press, 1976), Alfred David argues that *The Canterbury Tales* is in part a statement about the moral limitations of art. John M. Fyler makes a somewhat similar point in his perceptive study of the affinities between Chaucer's sensibility and Ovid's: "Each turns repeatedly to a basic epistemological problem: the extent to which the artist, or indeed any human being, is capable of setting up structures of perception and understanding that are true, or at least sufficiently trustworthy to permit effective action in the world. Each answers the problem by leaving it unresolved"—*Chaucer and Ovid* (New Haven: Yale University Press, 1979), p. 20. The notion that Chaucer in *The Canterbury Tales* questions the validity of literary art becomes a major theme in Cooper's *The Structure of the Canterbury Tales* (see especially pp. 55, 161-207, 240). Paul Christianson, "Chaucer's Literacy," *Chaucer Review*, 11 (1976), 112-27, studies Chaucer's notion of literacy, and concludes that Chaucer is often a bit skeptical about the validity of language. Russell A. Peck, "Chaucer and the Nominalist Question," *Speculum*, 53 (1978), explores the possibility that Chaucer was familiar with the linguistic theories of Ockham and other nominalists, and Peck says that Chaucer is "nominalist" like Ockham in his "basic awareness of the limitations of all kinds of demonstration and the relative importance of differentiating between the linguistic realities of their study and the greater reality of the things being studied" (p. 760). In this connection see also Norman T. Harrington, "Experience, Art, and the Framing of the *Canterbury Tales*," *Chaucer Review*, 10 (1976), 187-200. Robert O. Payne discusses the "problem of poetry" in Chaucer; the Pardoner and the Parson represent "opposite ends of a continuum," where "At one pole, we have the bad man whose superlative skills not only work but produce good results; at the other, the good man whose unwillingness to falsify himself by any art vitiates his good intentions. The illusion succeeds better than the reality"—"Rhetoric in Chaucer: Chaucer's Realization of Himself as Rhetor," in James J. Murphy, ed., *Medieval Eloquence: Studies in the Theory and Practice of Medieval Rhetoric* (Berkeley: University of California Press, c1978), pp. 275-76. See also Ronald B. Herzman, "The Paradox of Form: *The Knight's Tale* and Chaucerian Aesthetics," *Papers on Language and Literature*, 10 (1974), 339-52.

Herzman says, "throughout *The Canterbury Tales* one is implicitly reminded of the insufficiency of art, and this concern is made explicit in the retraction" (p. 349). Evan Carton, "Complicity and Responsibility in Pandarus' Bed and Chaucer's Art," *PMLA*, 94 (1979), remarks in a study of the relation between Pandarus and the Chaucerian narrator that "Chaucer's fictional pilgrimage never reaches Canterbury and never was meant to reach it; instead, it explores the communal way, the unstable and impure world that we create through the stories we tell one another" (60). See also Martin Irvine, "Medieval Grammatical Theory and Chaucer's *House of Fame*," *Speculum*, 60 (1985), 850-76.

22 "In Defense of the Bradshaw Shift," *Chaucer Review*, 12 (1978), 198. Jill Mann and Derek Pearsall choose to look at the other side of this particular coin in their reviews of Howard's book. Mann, *Medium Aevum*, 47 (1978), 359, says that Howard's grouping of tales "is no more convincing than any produced by other critics and rejected by Howard, and it is no less imposed on the text from without than they are." Pearsall, *Modern Language Review*, 74 (1979), 156, argues that "the idea of multiple thematic structuring, as it is indulged here, is so far remote from control, purpose, and *form* that it is the very denial of form...."

23 *The Art of the Canterbury Tales* (Madison: University of Wisconsin Press, 1965), p. 251. See also Robertson, *A Preface to Chaucer*, p. 336.

24 *The Works of Geoffrey Chaucer*, 2nd edition, ed. F. N. Robinson (Boston: Houghton Mifflin, c1957), p. 229.

25 See, for example, John Finlayson, "The Satiric Mode and the *Parson's Tale*," *Chaucer Review*, 6 (1971), 111; Norman Harrington, "Experience, Art, and the Framing of the *Canterbury Tales*," p. 199; Paul Christianson, "Chaucer's Literacy," p. 123; Russell Peck, "Chaucer and the Nominalist Question," p. 758; and John M. Fyler, *Chaucer and Ovid*, p. 149. "Relativism" and, especially, "perspective" are the central notions in Cooper's reading of *The Canterbury Tales*: "Different genres arise from, and imply, very different ways of looking at the world or interpreting human experience.... In judging the tales one is also being compelled to judge the attitudes they embody." Chaucer will "explore the potential forms, look through those windows...; but by his consciousness that each gives a different view, and by giving each of those views in turn, he insists on the fact that they are only perspectives..." (*The Structure of the Canterbury Tales*, pp. 54-55).

NOTES TO CHAPTER THREE

1 Charles A. Owen, Jr., "The Plan of the Canterbury Pilgrimage," *PMLA*, 66 (1951), 825, suggests that the tales of the first day open with a presentation of the "chivalric ideal in love and war." Then the Miller presents his version of love and the Reeve presents his version of war. See also Robert Worth Frank, Jr., "The *Reeve's Tale* and the Comedy of Limitation," in *Directions in Literary Criticism: Contemporary Approaches to Literature*, Festschrift for Henry W. Sams, ed. Stanley Weintraub and Philip Young (University Park: Pennsylvania State University Press, c1973), pp. 53-69.

2 Robert Jordan, *Chaucer and the Shape of Creation: The Aesthetic Possibilities of Inorganic Structure* (Cambridge: Harvard University Press, 1967), p. 153,

points out the importance of rationality in the Knight's tale; whereas Howard, *The Idea of the Canterbury Tales*, points out the degenerative movement in the values placed on intellect in the successive tales of the fragment (p. 242).

3 John H. Fisher, "Chaucer's Last Revision of the *Canterbury Tales*," *Modern Language Review*, 67 (1972), 248.

4 Alfred David, *The Strumpet Muse*, pp. 95, 111.

5 E. D. Blodgett, "Chaucerian *Pryvetee* and the Opposition to Time," *Speculum*, 51 (1976), 489, 491.

6 *The Idea of the Canterbury Tales*, pp. 237, 240.

7 Charles Muscatine, "Form, Texture, and Meaning in Chaucer's *Knight's Tale*," *PMLA*, 65 (1950), 911-29; later incorporated into *Chaucer and the French Tradition: A Study in Style and Meaning* (Berkeley: University of California Press, 1957).

8 R. E. Kaske, "The Knight's Interruption of the *Monk's Tale*," *ELH*, 24 (1957), 261-63. See also John Halverson, "Aspects of Order in the Knight's Tale," *Studies in Philology*, 57 (1960), 606-21, for another argument that the tale is essentially Boethian, with Palamon and Arcite representing imperfect knighthood, and Theseus, the "agent and spokesman of social authority," representing mature, perfect knighthood. "The role of Theseus is like that of Philosophy" in Boethius, for Halverson.

9 Huppé, *A Reading of the Canterbury Tales*, p. 56, identifies Theseus as the "center of positive development" held up by the Knight before the Squire, and Palamon and Arcite as the "negative."

10 John M. Fyler, *Chaucer and Ovid*, pp. 128-29, 146-47. Richard Neuse works an interesting (though I think ultimately unconvincing) variation of the dramatic readings, in "The Knight: The First Mover in Chaucer's Human Comedy," *University of Toronto Quarterly*, 31 (1962), 299-315. Neuse argues that the Knight is "basically comic and ironic. We see him in an unbuttoned, holiday mood" (p. 300). Thus, though Neuse sees the tale as dramatic revelation of the Knight's character, he does not therefore conclude that Theseus' vision is valid. It might seem that Neuse's approach invalidates my thesis that it is characteristic of dramatic readings to take Theseus' vision as valid. But the real theoretical problem here is the problem of how one tells when there is irony. Many have seen some irony in the tale, but most have not seen the whole tale as ironic. An ironic reading is a kind of inversion, like putting a minus sign in front of an algebraic expression and thus changing all the values inside the parentheses. One might expect, then, that an ironic dramatic reading of the tale would invert the value of Theseus' vision. Terry Jones, *Chaucer's Knight: The Portrait of a Medieval Mercenary* (Baton Rouge: Louisiana State University Press, 1980), is another case in point. Jones puts the minus sign of irony not in front of the Knight's tale itself, but in front of the portrait of the Knight in the General Prologue. The Chaucerian irony there indicates that the Knight is in fact a savage mercenary. The tale, then, told in the *persona* of the "uncourtly, unphilosophical and totally unromantic professional soldier" (145) illustrates a misunderstanding of "the nature of courtly chivalry" (153); Theseus is the typical Italian tyrant, and his "First Mover" speech is a "travesty" of Boethius (202); so that the whole tale

becomes a "hymn to tyranny" (212). (I shall have more to say later about Theseus' "tyranny.") Jones' dramatic reading, then, refuses to accept the vision of order in the tale—but only because Jones invokes the concept of irony, thus inverting all the values in the expression.

[11] P. M. Kean, *Chaucer and the Making of English Poetry*, vol. II: *The Art of Narrative* (London: Routledge & Kegan Paul, 1972), 29.

[12] Alan T. Gaylord, "The Role of Saturn in the *Knight's Tale*," *Chaucer Review*, 8 (1974), 174-75.

[13] Traugott Lawler, *The One and the Many in the Canterbury Tales*, p. 94.

[14] Dale Underwood, "The First of *The Canterbury Tales*," *ELH*, 26 (1959), 459-62. See also Paul Ruggiers, *The Art of the Canterbury Tales*, pp. 156, 161.

[15] F. Elaine Penninger, "Chaucer's *Knight's Tale* and the Theme of Appearance and Reality in *The Canterbury Tales*," *South Atlantic Quarterly*, 63 (1964), says that Chaucer intended the tale and the Knight himself "to represent beautiful, even admirable, but nevertheless unreal models" (p. 399). Jordan, *Chaucer and the Shape of Creation*, makes the point about Chaucer's "lapses" into low style and homely metaphor (pp. 179-84). See also Alfred David, *The Strumpet Muse*, p. 88; and Howard, *The Idea of the Canterbury Tales*, p. 237. Elizabeth Salter, *Fourteenth-Century English Poetry: Contexts and Readings* (Oxford: Clarendon Press, 1983), attributes the inadequacies of the tale to Chaucer's own artistic failure in his attempt to adapt Boccaccio's story to deal with profound Boethian themes (see especially pp. 177-81).

[16] Kathleen A. Blake, "Order and the Noble Life in Chaucer's *Knight's Tale?*" *Modern Language Quarterly*, 34 (1973), 17-19.

[17] Blodgett, "Chaucerian *Pryvetee* and the Opposition to Time," 487.

[18] "The *Knight's Tale* as an Impetus for Pilgrimage," *Philological Quarterly*, 43 (1964), 526-37. Like Westlund, Carol V. Kaske emphasizes the "pagan" nature of the Knight's tale. In "Getting Around the Parson's Tale: An Alternative to Allegory and Irony," in Rossell Hope Robbins, ed., *Chaucer at Albany* (New York: Franklin, 1975), pp. 147-77, Kaske argues that Chaucer deliberately begins *The Canterbury Tales* with a pagan tale, "a deliberate limitation of somebody's perspective to that of reason and experience" (p. 158). Kaske compares Chaucer's judging of the pagan view with Dante's, as I shall do later: the Parson's tale is Beatrice to the Knight's Vergil (p. 159). Cooper, *The Structure of the Canterbury Tales*, also emphasizes that the Knight's tale is "pagan." Cooper praises Theseus for his "understanding of a higher divine providential principle"; but as one would expect of a thematic critic, she stresses that Theseus' interpretation is "limited" and "does not altogether resolve the problem" posed by the cruelty of Fortune and the malevolence of the gods in the poem (p. 100).

[19] In citing *The Canterbury Tales* I shall use *The Works of Geoffrey Chaucer*, 2nd edition, ed. F. N. Robinson (Boston: Houghton Mifflin, c1957), and I shall cite the ten fragments according to the Roman numerals used by Robinson and corresponding to the order of the tales in the Ellesmere manuscript.

[20] Howard, *The Idea of the Canterbury Tales*, p. 240.

[21] Alfred David, *The Strumpet Muse*, suggests that the Miller's tale is more than just a "travesty of chivalric ideals": it reverses asceticism and the "religion of

love" (p. 95), distrusts intellect, and opposes itself to the "exegetical impulse" of the medieval mind (p. 99).

[22] John H. Fisher, "The Three Styles of Fragment I of the *Canterbury Tales*," *Chaucer Review*, 8 (1973), 119-27.

[23] Richard Neuse, "The Knight: The First Mover in Chaucer's Human Comedy," p. 308.

[24] Howard, p. 240.

[25] David, *The Strumpet Muse*, p. 95; see also Charles A. Owen, Jr., *Pilgrimage and Storytelling in the Canterbury Tales: The Dialectic of "Ernest" and "Game"*, p. 106, and Traugott Lawler, *The One and the Many in the Canterbury Tales*, p. 95.

[26] Huppé, *A Reading of the Canterbury Tales*, reads the tale rather grimly, as the methods of "historical criticism" tend to force one to do. He suggests that the tale serves to reveal the "dark ignorance" of the Miller's soul, reveling in the "Babylonic confusion of a world where men seek only their pleasures" (p. 85). At the level of the individual tale, Huppé interprets dramatically— as, indeed, he does with the Knight's tale, when he says that the Knight's purpose is to instruct his son in Christian chivalry. As Huppé moves from the level of the individual tale, of course, he invokes a larger, thematic principle (*caritas*) to relate his dramatic readings of the tales to each other. The Miller himself, as *dramatis persona*, comes to represent something in the larger structure. For Paul Ruggiers, Trevor Whittock, and Alfred David, among others, the Miller's tale reveals not the Miller's ignorance but another possible way of looking at the world, a world-view that has its own (limited) validity, just like the Knight's world-view. Ruggiers, *The Art of The Canterbury Tales*, suggests that Chaucer moves from the "high romantic" of the Knight's tale to the "low comic," but Chaucer himself holds both views (pp. 57, 64-65). Whittock thinks that the "positives" of the Miller's tale are "largely embodied in Alisoun," who represents the "animal vigour of unspoilt creation" (*A Reading of the Canterbury Tales*, pp. 86-87). And David suggests that the tale is serious at one level, with the seriousness of "festive comedy," the truth of "fidelity to the vital principle of life" (*The Strumpet Muse*, p. 105). These latter three critics clearly start from a thematic orientation toward the tale.

[27] See Richard Neuse, "The Knight: The First Mover in Chaucer's Human Comedy," p. 308.

[28] David, p. 99.

[29] Whittock, *A Reading of the Canterbury Tales*, says that the Reeve's tale shows the "Bitterness, frustration, and ugliness" of life (p. 97). Owen, *Pilgrimage and Storytelling in the Canterbury Tales*, speaks of the Reeve's world as one of "spiritual corruption and economic maneuver," and of the Reeve himself as demonstrating a "sapless and efficient hypocrisy" (pp. 106-07).

[30] Whittock, p. 100, notes that the Reeve exhibits a kind of "Swiftian disgust" in his cold, inhuman descriptions of sex; Owen, p. 109, sees in the tale a "world where sex is not so important as economics." John H. Fisher, "The Three Styles of Fragment I of the *Canterbury Tales*," points out the "country talk and sexual hilarity" in the tale, maintaining that the tale "reveals neither sentiment nor intellect, but only animal passion" (p. 123).

[31] *The Strumpet Muse*, p. 112. David goes on to give the tale a dramatic application—the Reeve, a voluntary serf, joins the Host in hostility to the bourgeois Miller's swaggering. The fabliau is essentially an aristocratic genre, expressing scornful hostility toward the bourgeoisie (pp. 114-16).

[32] *Pilgrimage and Storytelling*, p. 106.

[33] See E. D. Blodgett, "Chaucerian *Pryvetee* and the Opposition to Time." Peter Brown, "The Containment of Symkyn: The Function of Space in the *Reeve's Tale*," *Chaucer Review*, 14 (1980), 225-35, analyzes the Reeve's use of literal and metaphorical space, but Brown's emphasis is rather different from mine. Robert Worth Frank, Jr., "The *Reeve's Tale* and the Comedy of Limitation," in *Directions in Literary Criticism: Contemporary Approaches to Literature*, Festschrift for Henry W. Sams, ed. Stanley Weintraub and Philip Young (University Park: Pennsylvania State University Press, c1973), pp. 53-69, also argues for the importance of space in the tale, but takes rather the opposite point of view from mine: "If the miller is willing to be playful concerning space, reducing it to a fiction, the narrative insistently demonstrates its inescapable reality" (64).

[34] Howard, p. 247. John H. Fisher, "Chaucer's Last Revision of the *Canterbury Tales*," p. 248, intimates that the Cook's tale is broken off deliberately, so that we are "brought up sharp," ready for the Man of Law's tale, which "gets the series started again on a higher level."

NOTES TO CHAPTER FOUR

[1] For example, Howard, p. 215; P. M. Kean, *Chaucer and the Making of English Poetry*, II: *The Art of Narrative*, 114-18; and Huppé, p. 95.

[2] "Getting Around the Parson's Tale," in *Chaucer at Albany*, p. 160.

[3] *The Art of the Canterbury Tales*, p. 173. Bernard I. Duffey, "The Intention and Art of *The Man of Law's Tale*," *ELH*, 14 (1947), points out that Constance "is definitely not made perfect through suffering...; she was rather carefully made perfect to begin with" (p. 186).

[4] *A Reading of the Canterbury Tales*, p. 108.

[5] *The Strumpet Muse*, p. 131.

[6] Duffey, "The Intention and Art of *The Man of Law's Tale*," argues that Chaucer *intended* to produce a "sentimental tale" to satisfy middle-class taste. By this hypothesis, Duffey explains both the emotionalism of the tale, and Chaucer's attempts to gloss over the improbabilities in the plot by the long digressions into biblical precedents for miraculous intervention (pp. 193, 189). Ruggiers, *The Art of the Canterbury Tales*, p. 224, calls these passages (with justice, I think) "extravagant and facile claims on behalf of providential control...." Edward Block, "Originality, Controlling Purpose, and Craftsmanship in Chaucer's *Man of Law's Tale*," *PMLA*, 68 (1953), like Duffey bases his study on a comparison of Chaucer's work with the source in Trivet, and maintains that Chaucer unsuccessfully tried to do two things with Constance: "In trying to make her more religious and at the same time more human, he was motivated by what is fundamentally an irreconcilable dualism of purpose" (p. 592). Stephen Manning, "Chaucer's Constance, Pale and Passive," *Chaucerian Problems and Perspectives: Essays Presented to Paul E. Beichner, C.S.C.*, ed. Edward Vasta and Zacharias P. Thundy (Notre

131

Dame: University of Notre Dame Press, c1979), makes a similar point. Manning argues that the fact that Christ seems to do everything "raises questions about Constance's free will ... and indeed tends to cancel out some of her awareness of the emotional cost of yielding to the divine will" (pp. 20-21). John A. Yunck, "Religious Elements in Chaucer's *Man of Law's Tale*," *ELH*, 27 (1960), 249-61; Robert Enzer Lewis, "Chaucer's Artistic Use of Pope Innocent III's *De Miseria Humane Conditionis* in the Man of Law's Prologue and Tale," *PMLA*, 81 (1966), 485-92; and Sheila Delany, "Womanliness in the *Man of Law's Tale*," *Chaucer Review*, 9 (1974), 63-71, all try with different emphases to show that the human interest of the story should be subordinated in interpretation to its religious theme. Walter Scheps, "Chaucer's Man of Law and the Tale of Constance," *PMLA*, 89 (1974), attempts to account for the tedium of conspicuously rhetorical passages of the tale (those stressing the themes of Fortune, free will, and miraculous intervention—those, in other words, that do most to create the tension in our experience of the tale) by attributing to the passages a dramatic function. The Man of Law is showing off his rhetorical skill as a lawyer, and the tale is intended, by its teller, to be "an encomium upon the teller's profession" (p. 285).

[7] "Chaucer's Constance: Womanly Virtue and the Heroic Life," *Chaucer Review*, 13 (1979), 232.

[8] See Dorothy Bethurum Loomis, "*Constance and the Stars*," in Vasta and Thundy, ed., *Chaucerian Problems and Perspectives*, pp. 209 ff.

[9] Clasby, p. 223.

[10] On the crudity of this and other passages in the tale, see Sheila Delaney, "Womanliness in the *Man of Law's Tale*," pp. 65-67.

NOTES TO CHAPTER FIVE

[1] H. B. Hinckley, "The Debate on Marriage in the *Canterbury Tales*," *PMLA*, 32 (1917), 292-305; Clifford P. Lyons, "The Marriage Debate in the *Canterbury Tales*," *ELH*, 2 (1935), 252-62; Kemp Malone, "*The Wife of Bath's Tale*," *Modern Language Review*, 57 (1962), 489. Allen and Moritz, *A Distinction of Stories*, reorder the fragments, destroying the integrity of Kittredge's "Marriage Group" (pp. 137 ff.).

[2] William Witherle Lawrence, *Chaucer and the Canterbury Tales* (New York: Columbia University Press, 1950), pp. 122-23, and R. A. Pratt, "The Order of the *Canterbury Tales*," *PMLA*, 66 (1951), 1158, both adopt the Bradshaw shift, Lawrence including the *Melibeus* and Nun's Priest tale in the Marriage Group, and Pratt adding also the Monk's performance. Germaine Dempster, "A Period in the Development of the Canterbury Tales Marriage Group and of Blocks B² and C," *PMLA*, 68 (1953), 1142-59, includes the *Melibeus*, the *Melibeus*-Monk link, and the Nun's Priest's tale.

[3] For example, Margaret Schlauch, "The Marital Dilemma in the *Wife of Bath's Tale*," *PMLA*, 61 (1946), limits the Marriage Group to fragments III and IV (p. 430), and Clair C. Olson, "The Interludes of the Marriage Group in the *Canterbury Tales*," in Beryl Rowland, ed., *Chaucer and Middle English Studies in Honor of Rossell Hope Robbins* (Kent State University Press, 1974), removes the Merchant's tale from the group (pp. 165-66).

[4] "Chaucer's Marriage Group," in *Chaucer the Love Poet*, ed. Jerome Mitchell and William Provost (Athens: University of Georgia Press, c1973), pp. 45-65.

[5] See Gertrude M. White, "The Franklin's Tale: Chaucer or the Critics," *PMLA*, 89 (1974), 454-62, for a discussion of the themes of *gentilesse, trouthe, freedom, curteisie*, and *honour* in the Marriage Group and in other tales. See also Cooper, *The Structure of the Canterbury Tales*, pp. 124-25.

[6] D. W. Robertson, Jr., *A Preface to Chaucer*, p. 375.

[7] P. M. Kean, *Chaucer and the Making of English Poetry*, II: *The Art of Narrative*, 111.

[8] Robertson, p. 377. P. R. Szittya, "The Green Yeoman as Loathly Lady: The Friar's Parody of the *Wife of Bath's Tale*," *PMLA*, 90 (1975), 386-94, wants to see the Friar's and Summoner's tales as parts of the Marriage Group, by considering the group as a more general "debate about the proper foundation for human relationships" (p. 392).

[9] Howard's reading of these fragments as "Tales of Domestic Conduct," with a digressive movement whereby the Wife shifts from the issue of Constance's perfection to the issue of *maistrie* and the issue of a woman's wishes (*The Idea of the Canterbury Tales*, p. 255), seems to me one of the least satisfactory aspects of his book, however perceptive his readings of the individual tales are.

[10] Huppé, *A Reading of the Canterbury Tales*, p. 107; and Whittock, *A Reading of the Canterbury Tales*, p. 118, are examples.

[11] "A Question of Order in the *Canterbury Tales*," *Chaucer Review*, 1 (1966-67), 240-52; quotation from p. 248.

[12] George R. Coffman, "Chaucer and Courtly Love Once More—The Wife of Bath's Tale," *Speculum*, 20 (1945), 43-50, points out that in some sources it is clear that by the code of courtly love, peasant girls were fair game for "lusty bachelors." Huppé, "Rape and Woman's Sovereignty in the *Wife of Bath's Tale*," *Modern Language Notes*, 63 (1948), 378-81, extends the argument: the queen's point in her riddle is to decide whether the knight's action is excusable as a mere violation of the principle of *mesure*, or whether the knight fails to understand the basic principle of the sovereignty of women.

[13] Robert P. Miller, "*The Wife of Bath's Tale* and Medieval Exempla," *ELH*, 32 (1965), 442-56, sees the tale as a kind of anti-clerical exemplum, "educative and revelatory" (p. 452).

[14] Alfred David, *The Strumpet Muse*, p. 155; Paul Ruggiers, *The Art of the Canterbury Tales*, pp. 214-15.

[15] "The Green Yeoman as Loathly Lady: The Friar's Parody of the *Wife of Bath's Tale*," *PMLA*, 90 (1975), 386-94.

[16] Paul E. Beichner, "Baiting the Summoner," *Modern Language Quarterly*, 22 (1961), 371; Paul N. Zietlow, "In Defense of the Summoner," *Chaucer Review*, 1 (1966), 7-9; R. T. Lenaghan, "The Irony of the *Friar's Tale*," *Chaucer Review*, 7 (1973), 285.

[17] *A Preface to Chaucer*, p. 268.

[18] Huppé, *A Reading of the Canterbury Tales*, p. 199; Janet Richardson, "Friar and Summoner, The Art of Balance," *Chaucer Review*, 9 (1975), 235.

[19] Hugh L. Hennedy, "The Friar's Summoner's Dilemma," *Chaucer Review*, 5 (1971), 215; Charles A. Owen, Jr., *Pilgrimage and Storytelling in the Canterbury Tales*, p. 159.

20 Whittock, *A Reading of the Canterbury Tales*, p. 134; Richard H. Passon, "'Entente' in Chaucer's *Friar's Tale*," *Chaucer Review*, 2 (1968), 166-71.

21 *The Art of the Canterbury Tales*, p. 93.

22 Charles A. Owen, Jr., *Pilgrimage and Storytelling in the Canterbury Tales*, p. 96; Ruggiers, *The Art of the Canterbury Tales*, p. 167; Richardson, "Friar and Summoner, The Art of Balance," p. 234.

23 Bernard S. Levy, "Biblical Parody in the *Summoner's Tale*," *Tennessee Studies in Literature*, 11 (1966), 45-60; Alan Levitan, "The Parody of Pentecost in Chaucer's *Summoner's Tale*," *University of Toronto Quarterly*, 40 (1971), 236-46; P. R. Szittya, "The Friar as False Apostle: Antifraternal Exegesis and the *Summoner's Tale*," *Studies in Philology*, 71 (1974), 19-46. On the general question of Chaucer's attitude toward the friars in his works, see also Arnold Williams, "Chaucer and the Friars," *Speculum*, 28 (1953), 499-513, rpt. in Richard J. Schoeck and Jerome Taylor, ed., *Chaucer Criticism*, vol. I: *The Canterbury Tales* (Notre Dame: Notre Dame University Press, c1960), 63-83.

24 "By Preeve Which That is Demonstratif," *Chaucer Review*, 12 (1977), 81. On the theme of *experience* in the fragment, see also Cooper, *The Structure of the Canterbury Tales*, p. 133.

25 Robertson, *A Preface to Chaucer*, p. 273.

26 Whittock, *A Reading of the Canterbury Tales*, p. 139, stresses Friar John's blasphemy.

27 S. K. Heninger, Jr., "The Concept of Order in Chaucer's *Clerk's Tale*," *JEGP*, 56 (1957), 393, argues that the Clerk's primary purpose is religious; Charles Muscatine, *Chaucer and the French Tradition*, p. 194, points out that the theme of sovereignty is dealt with not only on the marital level, but also on the filial level and the political and religious levels; Ruggiers, *The Art of the Canterbury Tales*, p. 220, makes a similar observation.

28 Kemp Malone, "*The Wife of Bath's Tale*," *Modern Language Review*, 57 (1962), 490; Huppé, *A Reading of the Canterbury Tales*, p. 145; Kean, *Chaucer and the Making of English Poetry*, II: *The Art of Narrative*, 123; Lynn Staley Johnson, "The Prince and his People: A Study of the Two Covenants in the *Clerk's Tale*," *Chaucer Review*, 10 (1975), 19-20; David, *The Strumpet Muse*, pp. 163-64; Allen and Moritz, *A Distinction of Stories*, p. 192.

29 Joseph E. Grennen, "Science and Sensibility in Chaucer's Clerk," *Chaucer Review*, 6 (1971), 81-93, argues that the debate between the Wife and the Clerk is a debate about ways of getting knowledge—the nominalistic *via experientiae* advocated by the Wife, versus the realistic *via rationis* of the Clerk. The Clerk's tale then appears as an elaborate "sophism," or thought-experiment—as the Host says to the Clerk, "I trowe ye studie aboute som sophyme." I of course think that the world-view of the Clerk admits more validity in the *via experientiae* than Grennen allows.

30 S. K. Heninger, Jr., "The Concept of Order in Chaucer's *Clerk's Tale*," p. 391n, points out that Griselda is tested not for patience, but for constancy to her vow.

31 Grennen, "Science and Sensibility in Chaucer's Clerk," p. 91. John P. McCall, "*The Clerk's Tale* and the Theme of Obedience," *Modern Language Quarterly*, 27 (1966), 260-69, however, agrees with me that "by the free and

total submission of the human will, the will itself becomes sovereign" in the tale (261).

32 *A Reading of the Canterbury Tales*, pp. 143, 152. Whittock makes the Wife into a figure like Blake's Pebble and Griselda into a figure like Blake's Clod.

33 So James Sledd, "The *Clerk's Tale*: The Monsters and the Critics," *Modern Philology*, 51 (1953-54), 73-82, rpt. in Schoeck and Taylor, ed., *Chaucer Criticism*, I.160-74; and Robert M. Jordan, *Chaucer and the Shape of Creation*, p. 204; as well as several of the studies mentioned earlier.

34 Dolores Warwick Frese, "Chaucer's *Clerk's Tale*: The Monsters and the Critics Reconsidered," *Chaucer Review*, 8 (1973), iv, 138; Alfred David, *The Strumpet Muse*, p. 169.

35 Paul A. Olson, "Chaucer's Merchant and January's 'Hevene in erthe heere,'" *ELH*, 28 (1961), 214; Whittock, *A Reading of the Canterbury Tales*, p. 153; R. E. Kaske, "Chaucer's Marriage Group," in *Chaucer the Love Poet*, ed. Mitchell and Provost, pp. 45-65; Howard, *The Idea of the Canterbury Tales*, p. 264; see also Bertrand H. Bronson, *In Search of Chaucer* (Toronto: University of Toronto Press, 1960), p. 64. Several critics have argued that the Merchant's tale is an answer to the Wife as well as to the Clerk. See John H. Fisher, "Chaucer's Last Revision of the *Canterbury Tales*," *Modern Language Review*, 67 (1972), 249; Huppé, *A Reading of the Canterbury Tales*, p. 148; and Bernard S. Levy, "*Gentilesse* in Chaucer's *Clerk's* and *Merchant's Tales*," *Chaucer Review*, 11 (1977), 306-18.

36 Robert M. Jordan, "The Non-Dramatic Disunity of the *Merchant's Tale*," *PMLA*, 78 (1963), 293-99.

37 E. Talbot Donaldson, "The Effect of the Merchant's Tale," in *Speaking of Chaucer* (London: Athlone Press, University of London, c1970), pp. 37, 44-45; Norman T. Harrington, "Chaucer's Merchant's Tale: Another Swing of the Pendulum," *PMLA*, 86 (1971), 25-31; and I would also put Emerson Brown, Jr., in this category, though his article is entitled "Chaucer, The Merchant, and Their Tale: Getting Beyond Old Controversies"—see Part I, *Chaucer Review*, 13 (1978), 141-56, and Part II, *Chaucer Review*, 14 (1979), 247-62.

38 Martin Stevens, "'And Venus Laugheth': An Interpretation of the *Merchant's Tale*," *Chaucer Review*, 7 (1972), 125, 129.

39 See James I. Wimsatt, "Chaucer and the Canticle of Canticles," in *Chaucer the Love Poet*, ed. Mitchell and Provost, pp. 66-90.

40 Paul A. Olson, "Chaucer's Merchant and January's 'Hevene in erthe heere,'" pp. 205, 207.

41 Traugott Lawler, *The One and the Many in the Canterbury Tales*, p. 70, points out this similarity.

42 "The Crucial Passages in Five of the *Canterbury Tales*: A Study in Irony and Symbol," *JEGP*, 52 (1953), 300. See also Owen, *Pilgrimage and Storytelling*, pp. 190-91.

43 See Gertrude M. White, "'Holynesse or Dotage': The Merchant's January," *Philological Quarterly*, 44 (1965), 397-404, for an argument that religious "fantasye" is the "key to January's character." Cooper, *The Structure of the Canterbury Tales*, also points out January's perverse failure to learn from experience (pp. 141, 143).

44 "Chaucer's *Merchant's Tale*," *Modern Philology*, 33 (1935-36), 367-81; rpt. in Schoeck and Taylor, ed., *Chaucer Criticism*, I:175-89. The quotation is from p. 182.

45 *A Reading of the Canterbury Tales*, p. 162.

46 *The Strumpet Muse*, p. 179.

47 "Chaucer, the Merchant, and Their Tale: Getting Beyond Old Controversies," Part II, *Chaucer Review*, 14 (1979), 249, 257.

48 Marie Neville, "The Function of the *Squire's Tale* in the Canterbury Scheme," *JEGP*, 50 (1951), 168; John W. Clark, "*Does the Franklin Interrupt the Squire?*" *Chaucer Review*, 7 (1972), 160-61.

49 Derek Pearsall, "The Squire as Story-Teller," *University of Toronto Quarterly*, 34 (1964), 82-92.

50 Joyce E. Peterson, "The Finished Fragment: A Reassessment of *The Squire's Tale*," *Chaucer Review*, 5 (1970), 62-74. See also Charles F. Duncan, Jr., "'Straw for Youre Gentilesse': The Gentle Franklin's Interruption of the Squire," *Chaucer Review*, 5 (1970), 161-64.

51 Pearsall, Duncan, and others make this point. See especially Robert S. Haller, "Chaucer's *Squire's Tale* and the Uses of Rhetoric," *Modern Philology*, 62 (1965), 285-95.

52 See Whittock, *A Reading of the Canterbury Tales*, p. 164.

53 Neville, pp. 169-70, 177; Stanley J. Kahrl, "Chaucer's *Squire's Tale* and the Decline of Chivalry," *Chaucer Review*, 7 (1973), 194-209; Howard, *The Idea of the Canterbury Tales*, p. 267.

54 Neville, p. 168; Clair C. Olson, "The Interludes of the Marriage Group in the *Canterbury Tales*," in Beryl Rowland, ed., *Chaucer and Middle English Studies in Honor of Rossell Hope Robbins* (Kent State University Press, 1974), pp. 170-71; and Cooper, *The Structure of the Canterbury Tales*, p. 147.

55 Whittock, *A Reading of the Canterbury Tales*, pp. 164-65.

56 Howard, *The Idea of the Canterbury Tales*, p. 267.

57 Haller, "Chaucer's *Squire's Tale* and the Uses of Rhetoric," pp. 286, 288.

58 Whittock, p. 168.

59 Harry Berger, Jr., "The F-Fragment of the *Canterbury Tales*," Part I, *Chaucer Review*, 1 (1966-67), 94.

60 Whittock, p. 166; John P. McCall, "The Squire in Wonderland," *Chaucer Review*, 1 (1966), 105.

61 McCall, p. 108.

62 Alan T. Gaylord, "The Promises in *The Franklin's Tale*," *ELH*, 31 (1964), 331-65, argues that the Franklin does not really grasp the concept of *trouthe*. Chauncey Wood, "Of Time and Tide in the *Franklin's Tale*," *Philological Quarterly*, 45 (1966), 688-711, concludes that the Franklin's "infatuation" with the romance-world is being satirized. Anthony E. Luengo, "Magic and Illusion in *The Franklin's Tale*," *JEGP*, 77 (1978), 1-16, suggests that the Franklin is morally deficient, ignorant of court entertainment and contemporary thought about magic, and prone to make of *gentilesse* "nothing more than... face-saving, empty respectability" (p. 16).

[63] Ruggiers sees the contrast between the Merchant's tale and the Franklin's as the "antithesis that exists between the bitterly, unassailably true, and that more harmonious and optimistic vision which qualifies as a higher kind of truth" (*The Art of the Canterbury Tales*, p. 237). Whittock thinks that, though Chaucer sees the limits of the Franklin's vision, he endorses that vision more than he does that of most of the pilgrims (*A Reading of the Canterbury Tales*, p. 170). Lindsay A. Mann, "'Gentilesse' and the Franklin's Tale," *Studies in Philology*, 63 (1966), 10-29, shows how the tale is a "full dramatization and fleshing out" of the ideal of *gentilesse*. Gertrude M. White, "The Franklin's Tale: Chaucer or the Critics," *PMLA*, 89 (1974), 454-62, concentrates on the concept of *trouthe* in the tale, arguing that we have "the explicit declaration of a moral ideal, consonant with Christianity though not identified with it" (p. 460). Cooper, *The Structure of the Canterbury Tales*, points out that the tale could represent an ideal even if the Franklin misunderstands the ideal; for Cooper, with her generic orientation, the ideal portrayed is that of romance, as opposed to the cynicism of the Merchant's pseudo-romance (pp. 149-50). These readings, while admitting that the tale represents an ideal (and therefore a state of affairs not always, perhaps not ever, attained in real life), emphasize the validity of that ideal considered in itself.

[64] Interpretations attempting to reconcile the opponents in this controversy about the Franklin's tale might have merit as new interpretations. But as long as they are based on the assumption that the controversy is about "how the tale is," they cannot address the fundamental issue. R. E. Kaske's interpretation is a case in point. "Chaucer's Marriage Group," in *Chaucer the Love Poet*, ed. Mitchell and Provost, pp. 45-65, argues that Arveragus' apparently absurd or immoral action in sending Dorigen to Aurelius is actually the action of a wise and idealistic man who foresees Aurelius's repentance and wants to teach his charming but somewhat flighty wife a lesson in prudence. Kaske concludes that the tale does exhibit an ideal balance between husband and wife; but, with an admirable sense of the bounds of his own argument, Kaske also leaves open the possibility that Chaucer is ironic—that Chaucer is suggesting that the balance does not often come about in the real world (p. 65). Thus, Kaske recognizes that "explaining" Arveragus' action, so as to preserve the tale as the portrayal of an ideal, still does not solve the question of whether the world-view of the tale is valid (endorsed by Chaucer) or limited (made fun of by Chaucer). That question is not a genuine question, first because the alternatives are not exclusive, and second, because it is not a question about the tale. It is a question about the interpretive system that is being applied to the tale.

[65] Harry Berger, Jr., "The F-Fragment of the *Canterbury Tales*," *Chaucer Review*, 1 (1966-67), Part I, 88-102, and Part II, 135-56, also sets aside the question of the marriage-debate, in an article that in theoretical terms (though not in detail, certainly) takes an approach similar to my own.

[66] Berger, p. 155; Whittock, p. 170; White, p. 460; David, *The Strumpet Muse*, p. 183.

[67] Berger, p. 155.

[68] See W. Bryant Bachman, Jr., "'To Maken Illusioun': The Philosophy of Magic and the Magic of Philosophy in the *Franklin's Tale*," *Chaucer Review*, 12 (1977), 55-67.

[69] Gerhard Joseph, "The *Franklin's Tale*: Chaucer's Theodicy," *Chaucer Review*, 1 (1966), 28.

[70] Edwin B. Benjamin, "The Concept of Order in the Franklin's Tale," *Philological Quarterly*, 38 (1959), 122.

[71] James Sledd, "Dorigen's Complaint," *Modern Philology*, 45 (1947), 36-45, argues that the complaint is a "deliberate bit of rhetorical extravagance." Donald C. Baker, "A Crux in Chaucer's *Franklin's Tale*: Dorigen's Complaint," *JEGP*, 60 (1961), 56-64, contends that the exempla are carefully organized to correspond to Dorigen's possible courses of action, and that Dorigen's recitation leaves her in "exhausted indecision." Gerald Morgan, "A Defence of Dorigen's Complaint," *Medium Aevum*, 46 (1977), 77-97, says that the complaint is not an instance of psychological realism, but of literary decorum.

[72] Gerhard Joseph, "The *Franklin's Tale*: Chaucer's Theodicy."

[73] *The Art of the Canterbury Tales*, p. 236.

[74] "'To Maken Illusioun': The Philosophy of Magic and the Magic of Philosophy in the *Franklin's Tale*," pp. 61-64.

[75] *The Strumpet Muse*, p. 192.

NOTES TO CHAPTER SIX

[1] Owen, *Pilgrimage and Storytelling*, p. 183.

[2] Ruggiers, *The Art of the Canterbury Tales*, p. 123; Gerhard Joseph, "The Gifts of Nature, Fortune, and Grace in the *Physician's*, *Pardoner's*, and *Parson's Tales*," *Chaucer Review*, 9 (1975), 237-45; and R. Michael Haines, "Fortune, Nature, and Grace in Fragment C," *Chaucer Review*, 10 (1976), 220-35.

[3] Whittock, *A Reading of the Canterbury Tales*, p. 179; Joseph, p. 240. For a discussion of Chaucer's use of the technique of "exemplary" narrative, see Ann Middleton, "The *Physician's Tale* and Love's Martyrs: 'Ensamples mo than ten' as a Method in the *Canterbury Tales*," *Chaucer Review*, 8 (1973), 9-31.

[4] Joseph, p. 240; Richard L. Hoffman, "Jephthah's Daughter and Chaucer's Virginia," *Chaucer Review*, 2 (1967), 29.

[5] Peter G. Beidler, "The Pairing of the *Franklin's Tale* and the *Physician's Tale*," *Chaucer Review*, 3 (1969), 278.

[6] Beidler, p. 277, points out this contrast.

[7] See Lee C. Ramsey, "'The Sentence of it Sooth Is': Chaucer's *Physician's Tale*," *Chaucer Review*, 6 (1972), 197.

[8] Thomas B. Hanson, "Chaucer's Physician as Storyteller and Moralizer," *Chaucer Review*, 7 (1972), 137-38.

[9] Hanson, p. 138; P. M. Kean, *Chaucer and the Making of English Poetry*, II.183; Ramsey, p. 195.

[10] Joseph, p. 241; Haines, p. 225.

[11] *A Reading of the Canterbury Tales*, p. 183.

[12] Ramsey, p. 194.

[13] *The Idea of the Canterbury Tales*, p. 334.

[14] "Governance in the *Physician's Tale*," *Chaucer Review*, 10 (1976), 316-25.

[15] C. G. Sedgwick, "The Progress of Chaucer's Pardoner, 1880-1940," *Modern Language Quarterly*, 1 (1940), 431-58, rpt. in Schoeck and Taylor, ed., *Chaucer*

Criticism, vol. I; John R. Halverson, "Chaucer's Pardoner and the Progress of Criticism," *Chaucer Review*, 4 (1970), 184-202; Beryl Rowland, "Chaucer's Idea of the Pardoner," *Chaucer Review*, 14 (1979), 140-54.

16 *The Idea of the Canterbury Tales*, p. 372.

17 E. Talbot Donaldson, "Chaucer's Three 'P's': Pandarus, Pardoner, and Poet," *Michigan Quarterly Review*, 14 (1975), 297-98, notices that the Pardoner pretends to create a world that is unlike his own world because the rioters get justice but the Pardoner himself gets away with his villainy. But at last, the Pardoner gets his comeuppance, and the world created in the sermon comes true.

18 Ruggiers, *The Art of the Canterbury Tales*, p. 126; and Donaldson, "Chaucer's Three 'P's,'" p. 292, emphasize the mystery of human evil and inexorable divine justice in the tale.

19 See Christopher Dean, "Salvation, Damnation, and the Role of the Old Man in the *Pardoner's Tale*," *Chaucer Review*, 3 (1968), 44-49.

NOTES TO CHAPTER SEVEN

1 Alan Gaylord, "*Sentence* and *Solaas* in Fragment VII of the *Canterbury Tales*: Harry Bailly as Horseback Editor," *PMLA*, 82 (1967), 226-27; Howard, *The Idea of the Canterbury Tales*, pp. 272, 283, 287; Owen, *Pilgrimage and Storytelling*, p. 113. The concern of fragment VII with literature becomes the main theme in Cooper's reading of the fragment; furthermore, for Cooper this concern extends outward from this fragment to encompass the rest of the work: "the encyclopaedic emphasis in the *Tales* draws all literary experience within its range, and so the analysis given in this section has implications for the whole work. Any final understanding of the *Canterbury Tales* must take into account the discussion of poetry contained in this fragment" (*The Structure of the Canterbury Tales*, p. 162).

2 Ruggiers, *The Art of the Canterbury Tales*, p. 88.

3 E. Talbot Donaldson, "The Effect of the Merchant's Tale," in *Speaking of Chaucer*, pp. 41-42.

4 See Paul Schneider, "'Taillynge Ynough': The Function of Money in the *Shipman's Tale*," *Chaucer Review*, 11 (1977), 201. Critics involved in the controversy include Albert H. Silverman, "Sex and Money in Chaucer's *Shipman's Tale*," *Philological Quarterly*, 32 (1953), 333-34; Janette Richardson, "The Façade of Bawdry: Image Patterns in Chaucer's *Shipman's Tale*," *ELH*, 32 (1965), 303-13; John C. McGalliard, "Characterization in Chaucer's *Shipman's Tale*," *Philological Quarterly*, 54 (1975), 1-18; and V. J. Scattergood, "The Originality of the *Shipman's Tale*," *Chaucer Review*, 11 (1977), 210-31.

5 Schneider, p. 206.

6 Janette Richardson, "The Façade of Bawdry," suggests that the animal-images indicate that the characters are lowering themselves in the chain of being by their wrong attitudes toward sex and commerce.

7 See Whittock, *A Reading of the Canterbury Tales*, p. 196; Peter Nicholson, "The 'Shipman's Tale' and the Fabliaux," *ELH*, 45 (1978), 585; and Owen, *Pilgrimage and Storytelling*, p. 116.

8 Silverman, pp. 331-33; Whittock, p. 200.

9 Scattergood, pp. 224, 227; Nicholson, p. 585; and, especially, George R. Keiser, "Language and Meaning in Chaucer's *Shipman's Tale*," *Chaucer Review*, 12 (1978), 147-48. See also Cooper, *The Structure of the Canterbury Tales*,

pp. 164-65. Cooper suggests that the punning is part of the process in the fragment of "undermining the fixed status of language" (p. 165).

10 *"Cosyn* and *Cosynage*: Pun and Structure in the *Shipman's Tale*," *Chaucer Review*, 11 (1977), 321. The citations in the *MED* for *cosyn* and *cosynage* do not support the hypothesis that Chaucer is punning here, as Abraham himself notes.

11 *Pilgrimage and Storytelling*, p. 116.

12 "The Effect of the Merchant's Tale," p. 42.

13 *The Art of the Canterbury Tales*, p. 80.

14 Florence Ridley has devoted an entire monograph to the subject. See *The Prioress and the Critics*, University of California English Studies, no. 30 (Berkeley and Los Angeles: University of California Press, 1965).

15 *The Strumpet Muse*, p. 210. On the question of Chaucer's supposed bigotry, see Albert B. Friedman, "The *Prioress's Tale* and Chaucer's Anti-Semitism," *Chaucer Review*, 9 (1974), 118-29.

16 Ruggiers, *The Art of the Canterbury Tales*, p. 179; Whittock, *A Reading of the Canterbury Tales*, p. 208; Friedman, p. 125; and Cooper, p. 167, all mention the Prioress' sentimentality. Fyler, *Chaucer and Ovid*, p. 157, talks about her "horrifying childish piety."

17 *A Reading of the Canterbury Tales*, p. 207.

18 *A Reading of the Canterbury Tales*, p. 204.

19 See, for example, Arthur K. Moore, "*Sir Thopas* as Criticism of Fourteenth-Century Minstrelcy," *JEGP*, 53 (1954), 532-45; and Walter Scheps, "Sir Thopas: The Bourgeois Knight, the Minstrel and the Critics," *Tennessee Studies in Literature*, 11 (1966), 35-43.

20 Huppé, *A Reading of the Canterbury Tales*, p. 236, says, "The sentence of the *Tale of Melibeus* is the sentence of the *Canterbury Tales*."

21 Paul Ruggiers, "Serious Chaucer: The *Tale of Melibeus* and the Parson's Tale," in *Chaucerian Problems and Perspectives: Essays Presented to Paul E. Beichner, C.S.C.*, ed. Edward Vasta and Zacharias P. Thundy (Notre Dame: University of Notre Dame Press, c1979), pp. 86, 88; Paul Strohm, "The Allegory of the *Tale of Melibee*," *Chaucer Review*, 2 (1967), 32-42; Charles A. Owen, Jr., "The *Tale of Melibee*," *Chaucer Review*, 7 (1973), 267-80; F. Elaine Penninger, "Chaucer's *Knight's Tale* and the Theme of Appearance and Reality in *The Canterbury Tales*," *South Atlantic Quarterly*, 63 (1964), p. 403.

22 See, for example, Lumiansky, *Of Sondry Folk*, pp. 85-95.

23 Howard, *The Idea of the Canterbury Tales*, p. 273.

24 *A Distinction of Stories*, p. 214.

25 Delores Palomo, "What Chaucer Really Did to Le Livre de Mellibee," *Philological Quarterly*, 53 (1974), 304-20, argues (inconclusively, I think) that Chaucer constructs in the *Melibeus* "a very subtle stylistic parody" of the "pretentious and undistinguished piece of bourgeois moralizing" (p. 306). Alan T. Gaylord, "The Moment of *Sir Thopas*: Towards a New Look at Chaucer's Language," *Chaucer Review*, 16 (1982), 311-29, makes a point similar to what I shall say about *Sir Thopas*: "instead of a parody of romance, it is more like a fantasia, . . . with humor more reflexive than referential" (p. 319).

26 On the reference of "litel tretys" (line 957) and "tretys lyte" (963) as it affects this interpretation of Chaucer's speech, see John W. Clark, "'This Litel

Tretys' Again," *Chaucer Review*, 6 (1971), 152-56; and, especially, Glending Olson, "A Reading of the *Thopas-Melibee* Link," *Chaucer Review*, 10 (1975), 147-53.

27 Olson, p. 151, points out that Chaucer, by giving himself the "most frivolous literary *jeu*" as well as the "most ponderously didactic" work, "in a sense tests out the limits of a maker's activity...."

28 Alfred David, *The Strumpet Muse*, p. 220—but David takes the *Melibeus* seriously, as a straight speech from Chaucer the author.

29 Howard sees the Prioress' tale and *Sir Thopas* as a pair, one exhibiting the Christian system of values, one the chivalric, but both "debased and mindless" (*The Idea of the Canterbury Tales*, p. 215).

30 R. E. Kaske, "The Knight's Interruption of the *Monk's Tale*," *ELH*, 24 (1957), 249-68, argues that it does not; Douglas L. Lepley, "The Monk's Boethian Tale," *Chaucer Review*, 12 (1978), 162-70, argues that it does.

31 Whittock, p. 218; Howard, p. 273; Owen, *Pilgrimage and Storytelling*, p. 131; Fyler, *Chaucer and Ovid*, p. 157; Allen and Moritz, *A Distinction of Stories*, p. 214. Cooper, *The Structure of the Canterbury Tales*, exalts the Monk's tale into a kind of antitype of the whole of *The Canterbury Tales*; it is everything that a story-collection should not be, "everything that the *Canterbury Tales* is not" (p. 48).

32 Edward Socola, "Chaucer's Development of Fortune in the *Monk's Tale*," *JEGP*, 49 (1950), 159-71, finds such a developing conception.

33 William C. Strange, "The Monk's Tale: A Generous View," *Chaucer Review*, 1 (1967), 167-80.

34 Donald K. Fry, "The Ending of *The Monk's Tale*," *JEGP*, 71 (1972), 355-68.

35 "*The Monk's Tale*: A Generous View," p. 175.

36 "Notes Towards a Theory of Tragedy in Chaucer," *Chaucer Review*, 8 (1973), 96.

37 For example: Huppé, *A Reading of the Canterbury Tales*, p. 183; John B. Friedman, "The *Nun's Priest's Tale*: The Preacher and the Mermaid's Song," *Chaucer Review*, 7 (1973), 250-66; D. E. Myers, "Focus and 'Moralite' in the *Nun's Priest's Tale*," *Chaucer Review*, 7 (1973), 210-20; A. Paul Shallers, "The 'Nun's Priest's Tale': An Ironic Exemplum," *ELH*, 42 (1975), 319-37; Saul Nathaniel Brody, "Truth and Fiction in the *Nun's Priest's Tale*," *Chaucer Review*, 14 (1979), 33-47; Morton W. Bloomfield, "The Wisdom of the Nun's Priest's Tale," in *Chaucerian Problems and Perspectives*, ed. Vasta and Thundy, pp. 70-82; and Ian Bishop, "*The Nun's Priest's Tale* and the Liberal Arts," *Review of English Studies*, n. s. 30 (1979), 257-67.

38 For example: Arthur T. Broes, "Chaucer's Disgruntled Cleric: The *Nun's Priest's Tale*," *PMLA*, 78 (1963), 156-62; Charles S. Watson, "The Relationship of the 'Monk's Tale' and the 'Nun's Priest's Tale,'" *Studies in Short Fiction*, 1 (1964), 277-88; Whittock, *A Reading of the Canterbury Tales*, pp. 234-36; Rodney K. Delasanta, "'Namoore of this': Chaucer's Priest and Monk," *Tennessee Studies in Literature*, 13 (1968), 117-32; and Charles A. Owen, Jr., "The Crucial Passages in Five of the *Canterbury Tales*: A Study in Irony and Symbol," *JEGP*, 52 (1953), 309, and *Pilgrimage and Storytelling*, p. 140.

39 "Patristic Exegesis in the Criticism of Medieval Literature: The Opposition," in *Speaking of Chaucer*, pp. 149-50; rpt. from *Critical Approaches to Medieval Literature: Selected Papers from the English Institute*, ed. Dorothy Bethurum (New York: Columbia University Press, 1960). See also Stephen

Manning, "The Nun's Priest's Morality and the Medieval Attitude Toward Fables," *JEGP*, 59 (1960), 416; Norman E. Eliason, *The Language of Chaucer's Poetry*, Anglistica 17 (Copenhagen: Rosenkilde and Bagger, 1972), p. 172; and Susan Gallick, "Styles of Usage in the *Nun's Priest's Tale*," *Chaucer Review*, 11 (1977), 244-45.

40 *Chaucer and Ovid*, p. 156.

41 Several critics stress the constant shifting of perspective. See, for example, Muscatine, *Chaucer and the French Tradition*, p. 239; David, *The Strumpet Muse*, p. 223; Howard, *The Idea of the Canterbury Tales*, p. 287; and Jill Mann, "The *Speculum Stultorum* and the *Nun's Priest's Tale*," *Chaucer Review*, 9 (1975), 278. Cooper, *The Structure of the Canterbury Tales*, makes the shifting of literary perspectives the essential point in her reading of the tale; and, since the tale is "an encapsulization of everything that the *Canterbury Tales* is" (p. 180) and its narrator is "the poet's double" (p. 184), the "relativism" insisted on in the tale is also the central theme of the whole work.

42 For various approaches to this question, see Broes, "Chaucer's Disgruntled Cleric," p. 162; Friedman, "The *Nun's Priest's Tale*: The Preacher and the Mermaid's Song," p. 261; and Bishop, "*The Nun's Priest's Tale* and the Liberal Arts," p. 262.

43 "The *Speculum Stultorum* and the *Nun's Priest's Tale*," p. 277.

44 Some think that Chaucer is mocking people who believe that literature has to have a clear, easily extractable moral that is statable in literal terms—so Manning, "The Nun's Priest's Morality and the Medieval Attitude Toward Fables," p. 416; R. T. Lenaghan, "The Nun's Priest's Fable," *PMLA*, 78 (1963), 306-07; and Gallick, "Styles of Usage in the *Nun's Priest's Tale*," p. 244.

45 Mann, p. 277.

46 Fyler, *Chaucer and Ovid*, p. 161, says that the Nun's Priest undercuts his claim for the seriousness of the morality "by repeatedly indicating the patent incongruity of the experience that the *Tale* presents with the form imposed upon it."

47 F. Anne Payne, "Foreknowledge and Free Will: Three Theories in the *Nun's Priest's Tale*," *Chaucer Review*, 10 (1976), 201-19, argues that in fact the Nun's Priest understands the views of Augustine, Boethius, and Bradwardine and is mocking them.

48 See Watson, "The Relationship of the 'Monk's Tale' and the 'Nun's Priest's Tale.'"

49 On Chaucer and nominalism, see Russell A. Peck, "Chaucer and the Nominalist Question," *Speculum*, 53 (1978), 745-60. P. B. Taylor, "Chaucer's Cosyn to the Dede," *Speculum*, 57 (1982), 315-27, discusses how Chaucer throughout *The Canterbury Tales* is "confronting contemporary philosophical, or theological, speculations about relationships between word, its informing thought, and its incited act" (p. 317). See also Stewart Justman, "Literal and Symbolic in the *Canterbury Tales*," *Chaucer Review*, 14 (1980), 199-214; and Martin Irvine, "Medieval Grammatical Theory and Chaucer's *House of Fame*," *Speculum*, 60 (1985), 850-76.

50 Howard R. Patch, "Troilus on Determinism," *Speculum*, 6 (1931), 243; Ida L. Gordon, *The Double Sorrow of Troilus: A Study of Ambiguities in* Troilus and Criseyde (Oxford: Oxford University Press, 1970), p. 45; P. M. Kean, *Chaucer and the Making of English Poetry*, I.141; and Ian Bishop, "*The Nun's Priest's Tale* and the Liberal Arts," p. 266.

51 Adrienne R. Lockhart, "Semantic, Moral and Aesthetic Degeneration in *Troilus and Criseyde*," *Chaucer Review*, 8 (1973), 116; Donaldson, "Chaucer's Three 'P's': Pandarus, Pardoner, and Poet," *Michigan Quarterly Review*, 14 (1975), 291; Howard, *The Idea of the Canterbury Tales*, p. 136; Rose A. Zimbardo, "Creator and Created: The Generic Perspective of Chaucer's *Troilus and Criseyde*," *Chaucer Review*, 11 (1977), 294-96; Thomas A. Van, "Chaucer's Pandarus as an Earthly Maker," *Southern Humanities Review*, 12 (1978), 89-97; Fyler, *Chaucer and Ovid*, pp. 130-38; and Evan Carton, "Complicity and Responsibility in Pandarus' Bed and Chaucer's Art," *PMLA*, 94 (1979), 47-61.

52 David, *The Strumpet Muse*, calls the tale a "late, wise, and affectionate reassessment of the poet's task" (p. 224) that emerges as a "satire on human learning," a "satire on the medieval art of composition as it is taught in the rhetoric books" (p. 225), and a satire on "pride in our human intelligence. This is especially the vanity of authors..." (p. 229).

NOTES TO CHAPTER EIGHT

1 See, for example, Joseph E. Grennen, "Saint Cecilia's 'Chemical Wedding': The Unity of the *Canterbury Tales*, Fragment VIII," *JEGP*, 65 (1966), 466-81; and Bruce A. Rosenburg, "The Contrary Tales of the Second Nun and the Canon's Yeoman," *Chaucer Review*, 2 (1968), 278-91. Alfred David, *The Strumpet Muse*, p. 236, argues that the pairing of the tales creates an analogy between "the alchemists and some poets."

2 *A Reading of the Canterbury Tales*, p. 254.

3 Carolyn P. Collette makes a similar point in her discussion of images of sight and blindness in the tale: "A Closer Look at Seinte Cecile's Special Vision," *Chaucer Review*, 10 (1976), 337-49. Collette points out that the etymologizing of St. Cecilia's name turns on St. Augustine's distinction between *thing* and *sign*.

4 Paul E. Beichner, C.S.C., "Confrontation, Contempt of Court, and Chaucer's Cecilia," *Chaucer Review*, 8 (1974), 204, says that Chaucer has "intensified the clash" between Cecilia and Almachius as it is portrayed in his sources.

5 *The Idea of the Canterbury Tales*, p. 304.

6 See Norman T. Harrington, "Experience, Art, and the Framing of the *Canterbury Tales*," *Chaucer Review*, 10 (1976), 192-93.

7 *Chaucer and the French Tradition*, p. 217.

8 "Saint Cecilia's 'Chemical Wedding': The Unity of the *Canterbury Tales*, Fragment VIII," *JEGP*, 65 (1966), 466-81.

9 "The Contrary Tales of the Second Nun and the Canon's Yeoman," *Chaucer Review*, 2 (1968), 278-91.

10 Several scholars have read the tale in the light of alchemical treatises of Chaucer's own time. Edgar H. Duncan, "The Literature of Alchemy and Chaucer's *Canon's Yeoman's Tale*: Framework, Theme, and Characters," *Speculum*, 43 (1968), 633-56, argues that Chaucer is writing in an anti-alchemical tradition. Rosenburg, "Swindling Alchemist, Antichrist," *Centennial Review*, 6 (1962), 566-80; and Grennen, "The Canon's Yeoman's Alchemical 'Mass,'" *Studies in Philology*, 62 (1965), 546-60, both argue that the alchemical "work" is a kind of blasphemous parody—of God's work of creation, or Christ's work of redemption, or the priest's work of transubstantiation.

11 See, for example, John Matthews Manly, "Chaucer and the Rhetoricians," *Proceedings of the British Academy*, 12 (1926), 95-113, rpt. in Schoeck and Taylor, ed., *Chaucer Criticism*, I.284; J. Burke Severs, "Is the *Manciple's Tale* a Success?" *JEGP*, 51 (1952), 1-16; William Cadbury, "Manipulation of Sources and the Meaning of the *Manciple's Tale*," *Philological Quarterly*, 43 (1964), 538-48; Jackson J. Campbell, "Polonius Among the Pilgrims," *Chaucer Review*, 7 (1972), 140-46; John C. Hirsh, "The Politics of Spirituality: The Second Nun and the Manciple," *Chaucer Review*, 12 (1977), 129-46; Stewart Justman, "Literal and Symbolic in the *Canterbury Tales*," *Chaucer Review*, 14 (1980), 212; and Cooper, *The Structure of the Canterbury Tales*, pp. 195-99. Cooper believes that the Manciple and the Parson reject *rhetoric* in favor of "an unadorned truth," thus destroying "the whole foundation upon which imaginative literature is built" (p. 195). I shall argue that the questioning goes much deeper here—not just what we would call "literature," but *language itself* is put to the question. If my reading is "right"—one might even say, if Cooper's own reading is "right"—then the concept of "unadorned truth" has itself become deeply problematic by the end of *The Canterbury Tales*. Also, whatever the Parson's tale salvages of the claims of language—and I think it does salvage something—it salvages for literature as well. The opposition between "literary" and "non-literary" is precisely what *The Canterbury Tales* calls into question.

12 "Language and the Real: Chaucer's Manciple," *Chaucer Review*, 6 (1972), 271.

13 *The Idea of the Canterbury Tales*, p. 305.

NOTES TO CHAPTER NINE

1 See Robert Jordan, *Chaucer and the Shape of Creation*, pp. 229, 240-41.

2 Fyler, *Chaucer and Ovid*, p. 154, notes how the "mood of the last three Prologues becomes progressively more eerie."

3 See Alfred David, *The Strumpet Muse*, pp. 237-38.

4 Fyler, *Chaucer and Ovid*, p. 155.

5 Ruggiers, *The Art of the Canterbury Tales*, pp. 10-15. Carol V. Kaske, "Getting Around the Parson's Tale: An Alternative to Allegory and Irony," in Rossell Hope Robbins, ed., *Chaucer at Albany* (New York: Franklin, 1975), p. 159, suggests that the Parson's tale is the Beatrice to the Knight's Vergil.

6 David, *The Strumpet Muse*, pp. 237-38; Howard, *The Idea of the Canterbury Tales*, p. 386; Ruggiers, "Serious Chaucer: The *Tale of Melibeus* and the Parson's Tale," in *Chaucerian Problems and Perspectives*, ed. Vasta and Thundy, pp. 89-90.

7 Ruggiers, "Serious Chaucer," p. 90.

8 *A Reading of the Canterbury Tales*, p. 295.

9 David, *The Strumpet Muse*, p. 239, argues that the Retractation is a statement about the limitations of art: "In retracting his works Chaucer does not deny their right to exist, but he wants to warn us about the limitations of poetry lest they be misused, and he wants to be forgiven for the venial sin of having created something of such equivocal worth."

10 On the question of *compilatio* as a medieval genre, see Larry D. Benson, "The Order of *The Canterbury Tales*," *Studies in the Age of Chaucer*, 3 (1981), 112; and Cooper, *The Structure of the Canterbury Tales*, p. 57.

www.ingramcontent.com/pod-product-compliance
Lightning Source LLC
Chambersburg PA
CBHW060324050426
42449CB00011B/2644